Feast of Faith

This book is dedicated
to our children, Lucia and Chad,
who have helped us take
a closer walk with God.

Feast of Faith

Celebrating the Christian Year at Home

Kevin and Stephanie Parkes

The National Society
*Leading Education
with a Christian Purpose*
Church House Publishing

National Society/Church House Publishing
Church House
Great Smith Street
London SW1P 3NZ

ISBN 0 7151 4938 5

Published 2000 by National Society Enterprises Ltd

Cover design by Julian Smith

Printed in England by Biddles Ltd, Guildford and King's Lynn

Contents

Acknowledgements   vi

Introduction   vii

How to use this book   ix

Seasons of the Christian Year   1

    Advent   5

    Christmas   16

    Epiphany   19

    Candlemas   22

    Ash Wednesday – The first day of Lent   24

    Lent – The following weeks   26

    Annunciation of our Lord to the Blessed Virgin Mary   31

    Palm Sunday   33

    Maundy Thursday   36

    Good Friday   40

    Holy Saturday   42

    Easter Day   46

    Ascension   48

    Pentecost   50

    Trinity Sunday   53

    Corpus Christi   56

    Petertide   59

    The Transfiguration   63

    Michaelmas   65

    All Saints and All Souls   67

    Christ the King   70

    Further Liturgies   73

Appendix 1 – The lectionary year   80

Appendix 2 – The date of Easter and accompanying festivals   81

Appendix 3 – Resources   82

Acknowledgements

The publisher gratefully acknowledges permission to reproduce copyright material in this publication. Every effort has been made to trace and contact copyright holders. If there are any inadvertent omissions we apologize to those concerned and will ensure that a suitable acknowledgement is made at the next reprint. Page numbers are indicated in parentheses.

The Archbishops' Council of the Church of England: extracts from *The Alternative Service Book 1980* **(46, 59, 70)**; *Lent, Holy Week, Easter* (1986) **(36, 42-3)**; *The Promise of His Glory* (1991) **(6iv, 10, 12-13, 16, 19, 22i, 67ii)**; and *Common Worship: Services and Prayers for the Church of England* (2000) are copyright © The Archbishops' Council of the Church of England and reproduced by permission.

Board for Ministries, Diocese of Birmingham: material from the *Home Liturgies* pack © Board for Ministries, Diocese of Birmingham and used by permission **(73–9)**.

Cambridge University Press: Extracts adapted from *The Book of Common Prayer* (1662), the rights in which are vested in the Crown in the United Kingdom, are reproduced by permission of the Crown's Patentee, Cambridge University Press **(6 i-iii, 16, 19, 22ii, 24, 27 i, ii and iv, 31, 33, 40, 43, 48, 50, 53, 65, 67i)**.

Church of the Province of Southern Africa: *An Anglican Prayer Book 1989* © Provincial Trustees of the Church of the Province of Southern Africa **(27v)**.

Revd Robert J. Croker: Girl Guide World Hunger Grace. Words as used by the Hunger Task Force, Anglican Church of Canada, Diocese of Huron **(65)**.

Curtis Brown Ltd: recipe for Soul cakes is reproduced by permission of Curtis Brown Ltd, London, on behalf of Toni Arthur. Copyright © Toni Arthur 1981 **(69)**.

Episcopal Church of the USA, The Book of Common Prayer according to the use of the Episcopal Church of the USA, 1979. The ECUSA Prayer Book is not subject to copyright **(27iii)**.

The European Province of the Society of St. Francis: material from *Celebrating Common Prayer* (Mowbray, 1992) © The Society of St Francis is used with permission **(12)**.

General Synod of the Church of Ireland: *Collects and Post Communion Prayers*, 1995. Reproduced with permission **(63)**.

Granada Media Consumer Products: recipe for Vegetable hot pot from *Farmhouse Cookbook* (1975, p. 84) is copyright © Yorkshire Television and is reproduced courtesy of Granada Media Consumer Products **(25)**.

Gruner and Jahr: recipes for St Nicholas biscuits, Hot cross buns, Herby chicken pieces, Ascension cake, Fish bites and Michaelmas tart are reproduced courtesy of *Prima* magazine **(14, 41, 47, 49, 62, 66)**.

HarperCollins Publishers: recipe for Pashka from *The Supreme Vegetarian Cook Book* (Fontana Publishing, 1988) is copyright © Rose Eliot and is reproduced by permission of HarperCollins Publishers Ltd **(47)**.

Lion Publishing: 'The bread is warm and fresh' from *Everyday Graces* (Lion Publishing PLC, 1993) is reproduced with permission **(56)**.

McCrimmon Publishing Co. Ltd: extracts from *The Passover Meal* by H.J. Richards are copyright © McCrimmon Publishing Co. Ltd 1986 and are reproduced by permission **(38–9)**.

Oxfam Publishing: D. Dalton, T. Garlake, I. Taylor, *The Coffee Chain Game* (Oxfam Great Britain, 1994) and used by permission **(56–8)**.

Oxford University Press: extracts from 'O come, O come, Emmanuel', trans. T. A. Lacey (1853–1931) from *The English Hymnal* are reproduced by permission of Oxford University Press. Licence no. 05281.

RPL Ltd: recipe for Phulowrie and Candied sweet potatoes adapted from Polly E. Indar (ed.), *The Naparima Girls High School Recipe Book* (1988), p. 82 **(17-18)**.

Sheed and Ward Ltd: the Redemption Calendar from Oliver and Ianthe Pratt, *The Christmas and Easter Ideas Book* (1977) is reproduced by permission of the publishers **(28)**.

Somerfield Stores plc: recipe for Cheese and courgette tart from *Somerfield Magazine* (Summer, 1997) is reproduced with grateful thanks by permission of Somerfield Stores plc. **(35)**.

SPCK: 'Bless our home, Lord', from J. Carden (comp.), *Another Day*. Used by permission of the publishers **(48)**.

The United Reformed Church: 'O, thank you Lord', 'Roast potatoes; sticks and worms', 'Top nosh!' and 'O Lord, we're really grateful' from *Reign Dance*, © 1977 The Fellowship of United Reformed Youth and used by permission **(27, 33, 59, 67)**.

Wild Goose Publications: 'The summons', from *Heaven Shall Not Wait*. Words by John L. Bell and Graham Maule. Copyright © 1987 WGRG, Iona Community, 840 Govan Road, Glasgow, G51 3UU, Scotland **(60)**.

Woman's Own magazine: recipes for Farmhouse cake, Angel cake and Simnel cake, reproduced by permission **(21, 32, 45)**.

Introduction

This book has been written out of the experience of sharing faith with our own children. It is also in response to the many people we have met who have all asked similar questions: 'How can we share our faith in the home?' and, 'How can we help our children to grow up as Christians?'

As parents we set out to impart our faith to our children. We soon realized that our children were to teach us about God as well. We have learnt as parents that, like the Church, the family is on a faith journey together.

It is our understanding of the gospel that we are all called, whatever our age, to witness to those with whom we live. We know that we are called by God into discipleship, whatever our age. The lives of Jeremiah and Samuel show us this.

Within our family we, as adults, are helping our children to work out questions of faith for themselves. Families are not perfect, but we have found that if time and energy are given to them they can become places of transformation. Families can be places where we can be challenged and, like Jacob, wrestle with God.

The researcher into faith development, James Fowler, defined faith as that which we spend ourselves upon. We 'spend ourselves' on that which is important to us, whether it be football, making money, music, the latest fashion, keeping fit, or our religion.

If a parent had a passion for football and wanted to share this with the children, he or she would probably take the child to football matches, watch games on TV, read the sports pages in the newspapers, buy the football kit and meet with others with a passion for the game. In a similar way, a passion for faith can be shared with our children and with others.

In trying to share our faith we suggest that each family build upon what they already do, taking another step as it feels right to them. One way a family can do this is to look at the way they live and to ask themselves what changes can be made that would deepen and define the Christian faith in the home. What is experienced by adults and children in church can then be carried through into everyday life. There is a need for links to be made between life and faith and faith and life, between what happens at church and what happens at home, and between family members at worship and worship as a family. Links are also needed between what happens on a Sunday and what happens during the rest of the week.

We know that families come in many shapes and sizes – from the single parent family to the large extended group who may not be blood relatives. Whatever our idea of 'family', this book is offered to help the family of the Church give time to each other and to God.

The starting point for any family in faith must be with you, the parents and carers. It is important that the adults of the family discuss their faith commitment. It will then become clearer what you believe and what action you may want to take. This is especially important in families where only one parent has a religious faith commitment. Compromises will have to be reached that will be acceptable to all.

No two families are identical. There will be differences of opinions, of members, of ages, and of hopes and expectations.

In the Gospel of Luke (Chapter 18) we read of a young ruler who follows the religious laws. He comes to Jesus with a question, 'What more can I do?' Whatever our family is like, we follow his example and ask ourselves the question 'What more, as a family, can we do to deepen our faith and understanding?' We hope this book will help you find some answers to the question.

How to use this book

In each chapter you will find a number of sections:

✦ background information on the season or festival;

✦ the colour associated with it;

✦ suggested scripture readings, a prayer, and a grace to be used before a meal;

✦ ideas for preparing the home, ideas for activities, and some recipes;

✦ some questions to think about.

There are also Appendices and a Resource list at the back of the book for your additional use.

Each chapter may be used in its entirety, or a pick-and-mix approach may be used. The material is a collection of ideas and resources that we have used over the years. It is not meant to be prescriptive or a yardstick by which all families with children are to be measured. The book is a collection of our own experiences of sharing the faith in our home. It is intended to be a resource book to help you build upon the traditions you may already have in the home, such as celebrating birthdays, anniversaries, Christmas and Easter.

What follows is intended to help and encourage you to take the next step in faith within the family. Although the information and ideas can be used straight from the book, it is hoped that they will be used creatively and be a starting point for your own celebrations at home.

Although we, as adults, have instigated the celebrations, our children have contributed to their shape and form. Because of this, we have learned about God and what it is to have faith from our own children. We know to be true the saying that teachers are learners and learners are teachers!

The following are some suggestions as to how each section can be used.

The colour of the season or festival

Each season or festival day within the Church's year has a symbolic colour associated with it. This is used by the Church in various ways, including for altar frontals, banners and hangings, in the vestments that the clergy wear, and in flower arrangements. The colour of the season can be used in the home in various ways, including the candle at mealtime, the decoration of the home and the suggested activities for each season.

Background to the season or festival

We have included a brief history that may help to give a framework to your celebrations. There is also a description of how the Church interprets this through its traditions and worship. As an example of how the church celebration can be taken into the home we have included what we do in our own family.

Bible readings and prayers

In this section you will find readings taken from the Revised Common Lectionary, which your church may be following. The Lectionary gives Bible readings for each day of the year. We have included readings for particular festival days and for the Sundays during particular seasons such as Advent and Lent. Each group will include a reading from the Old Testament, the Epistles and the Gospels. These readings may be read in church and if used at home will provide a bridge between the two. A Bible reading can be used in different ways:

✦ It may be read by the adults to provide a scriptural basis for activities and themes of the festival.

✦ It can be read together, either before or during an activity in the home, to gain greater understanding.

◆ It can be read as part of the family meal.

◆ It can form part of the prayer time in the home.

◆ It can be read at bedtime.

With younger children it is important to tell a story as well as to read it. This will enable a young child to hear it in familiar words. Creative ways can be found to study the Bible together and discuss what it means and how it relates to today. Care should be taken to listen to each member of the group when they are relating their understanding and experiences. It is important that everyone is heard and feels that they have been listened to. A list of suitable Bibles for use with children may be found in the Resource list, p. 82.

The prayer is the 'collect' used in church near the beginning of the service to collect our thoughts and prayers before the Bible readings begin. Each of the prayers is quite long, so for younger children the prayer can be paraphrased or a few key words may be used. If the prayers are used regularly over the years they will become familiar and form part of the family's prayer life. The prayer can be used in a similar way to the Bible readings. Parents who feel self-conscious about praying with others may enjoy praying with the child at bedtime. As the child grows there may be an opportunity to set time apart for prayers when all the family can be together. In this time prayer can be offered for people and things that are of concern to you. Praying together gives each member of your family the opportunity to listen to each other's concerns and to hold each other before God. It also shows that it is an important activity, because adults are engaged in it. Creating a space for prayer is important – even if you don't have room for a permanent prayer space, you can create a space by lighting a candle and sitting around it or using an icon or a cross as a visual aid. Praying together may make you feel awkward at first. To help you, there are many books of prayers available, some of which are listed in the Resource list. Once you become familiar and comfortable with praying together you may not need the book anymore.

Grace before a meal

There are many reasons why some families do not eat together around a table on a regular basis. When this happens the family has lost one way of being together to discuss the day's events and make decisions as a family. The sharing of food lies at the heart of our faith. It is symbolic in many ways, especially of God's care and love. Family meals, whether daily or on Sundays, can be made special by saying a grace. Through the grace we give thanks to God for the food we eat and remember all our blessings. We remember also all those who suffer in the world for lack of food and water.

Each season and festival has been given a different grace that links with its theme. There are books of graces that will give you alternatives (these can be found in the Resource list, p. 83).

You may wish to make a grace card to be stood on the meal table for all to see. You will need:

> 1 piece of card 55 x 18 cm
> glue or sellotape
> scissors.

Make folds in the card at intervals of 16, 32 and 48 cm, leaving a strip of 7 cm. Write the grace on all three sides. Apply glue to the 7 cm strip and stick to the other end of the card to form a triangle.

Preparing the home

Homes are important places. They give a sense of identity and are expressions of who we are and the values we hold. I was once told a story of a young Jewish teacher who had recently moved to a new area, and had locked herself out of her flat. She telephoned the police and explained her situation and they obligingly sent two officers round to help her. One of them climbed up a drainpipe, in through an open window and then made his way down to let her in. 'The first thing he asked me,' she said, 'as he opened the door, was "Are you Jewish?" He had been in my flat no more than a minute and yet he had seen the one or two

how we learn and take in information. The activities we have included are intended to aid faith development – whatever our age. They are outward signs to help illustrate the meaning of our celebrations, which can communicate at many different levels.

Thoughts for food

When we think about the major events in our lives there is usually food and drink connected with them – at baptisms, weddings, funerals, birthdays, anniversaries, at welcomings and at departings. There is an expectation that food will be shared and we may feel cheated if there is not. Meals are important on many different levels. We accept other people's hospitality and we offer it ourselves as an expression of our relationship with them and of our connection to the particular event.

Sharing food is also central to our faith – for example, sharing the bread and wine at the eucharistic feast. There are elements of our celebrating the Eucharist in church that may help in our celebrations in the home:

♦ We gather – coming together as a group to eat is symbolic and has a power beyond the mere actions. We remember that meals were important to Jesus and ask that his presence bless the gathering and his peace will be what we share with one another.

♦ We share – those gathered recall past events. We do this in church every time we worship, recalling the story of our faith. In the home we may reflect upon what has happened in our day, and encourage one another to make links with family stories and stories from the Scriptures.

♦ We break bread – in church we participate in a eucharistic feast. Meal times at home also bring us all together to share in what others have made.

♦ We are sent – as we end our celebrations in church we are sent out to love and serve the world. In the home a simple prayer, blessing, gesture or song helps to send us back to our everyday lives.

things that, in their quiet way, proclaimed my religion.' She went on to say that this observation had so intrigued her that, whenever she visited a friend's home for the first time, she would look around to see if she could spot any sign that 'proclaimed' their religious practice. In the homes of Jewish, Muslim and Hindu friends there was usually some tell-tale sign, but in the homes of her Christian friends there was very rarely anything to suggest their religious beliefs. It is an interesting story. All too rarely do we see in the homes of Christian people anything that, even in a small way, quietly proclaims their faith. Some adults may feel self-conscious of any open display of beliefs, but this takes away the opportunity to witness to God in our family and to our friends. This can be done, not only by displaying religious artefacts, but by living out our faith in a meaningful way: living our lives with integrity as we try to live out our Christian faith. There is a marked difference between some Christian families, who do not mark even the major Christian festivals, with Jewish, Muslim and Hindu families who keep their religious festivals and root them in the home.

In this section we have included ideas that may help you to make your faith visible. This is particularly important for children to experience as they will take in information using all their senses.

Activities

The phrase 'I do, therefore I understand', used by some educationalists, is helpful in understanding

Gestures or ritual actions help us to participate without words. They allow us to express our 'felt needs' without saying anything. As we gather and share, simple actions may be used, for example the lighting of candles or the joining of hands.

We hope the recipes will help to make your celebrations special. Some of them you will be able to make with younger children, others will require more skill.

Food for thought

This section contains some questions connected to the theme of the day or season. They are intended as a help to the family to encourage thought and discussion. They can be reworded or kept as they are to be incorporated within the other sections.

Seasons of the Christian Year

Introduction

Most families will have traditions and festivals that they keep. Some will be common to all, such as celebrating birthdays, whilst others may focus around the marking of a particular event in the family's life. Festivals in the family remind us of the important events in its life.

In a similar way the Church also carries traditions and celebrates festivals, which are arranged into different seasons throughout the year. The new year for the Church begins on the first Sunday of Advent. Through the festivals and seasons of the year the Church directs our thoughts and worship to particular events in the life of Jesus.

The chart on the following page shows each of the seasons with a short explanation of their significance for us.

Name of the season	Significance	Symbolic colour
Advent	Advent is a season of preparation which begins on the closest Sunday to St Andrew's Day (which is celebrated on 30th November). Advent encourages us to prepare and make room for Jesus. There is expectancy, longing and desire for God to be given birth in our world.	Purple
Christmas	The Christmas season is the time in which we celebrate the birth of Jesus. God was made incarnate – being made flesh. Christmas Day marks the beginning of the twelve days of Christmas, otherwise known as Christmastide.	White or gold
Epiphany	The Epiphany is celebrated on 6th January each year. The word means 'showing'. During this season we remember how Jesus was revealed to the wise men and to the rest of the world. The days from 6th January to the beginning of Lent are known as Epiphanytide.	White or gold on 6th January. Green for the days leading up to Lent
Lent	Lent is another season of preparation. This season lasts 40 days, beginning on Ash Wednesday and ending on Holy Saturday, the day before Easter Day. The last week of Lent leading up to Easter Day is called Holy Week. This is when the last few days of Jesus' life are remembered. The season of Lent helps us to take a closer walk with God by looking to those things that hinder our love for him.	Purple
Easter	Easter Day marks the beginning of Eastertide. On Easter Day we celebrate the resurrection of Jesus from the dead. Every Sunday the resurrection of Jesus is celebrated and so becomes a re-enactment of Easter.	White or gold
Ascension	Ascension Day falls 40 days after Easter. Ascensiontide lasts for ten days.	White
Pentecost	The Day of Pentecost falls 50 days after Easter. At this time we remember the sending of the Holy Spirit upon the disciples of Jesus. Another name for this time is Whitsuntide.	Red
Trinity	The Sunday after Pentecost is called Trinity Sunday. This day reminds us that we worship one God who is Father, Son and Spirit.	White or gold
	The Sundays after Trinity Sunday are known as Sundays of Pentecost and help us to realize the presence and power of God in our world.	Green

Advent

Colour: purple

Background

The name Advent means 'coming'. The season holds together two themes – that of looking back and remembering the first coming of Christ and that of looking forward to Christ's second coming with all the themes of repentance, preparation and judgement.

The four Sundays in Advent lead us through our faith journey, beginning with the people who brought God's people together, then on to look at the prophets who called God's people to follow him more closely. The third Sunday looks at the prophetic call by John the Baptist to prepare and welcome the God of our salvation. This leads to the final Sunday of Advent with the focus on Mary, the mother of our Lord.

In our home we mark this season by the making of an Advent wreath and counting the days with an Advent calendar. We also like to use this time to create a Jesse Tree that uses the Bible to trace our faith story from Creation to the birth of Jesus. An opportunity to understand what God is already doing in the world is provided by the use of the 'O' antiphons in our home.

We have included some of these and other activities that you may like to include in your family preparations.

Bible readings

The First Sunday in Advent

YEAR A	YEAR B	YEAR C
Isaiah 2.1-5	Isaiah 64.1-9	Jeremiah 33.14-16
Romans 13.11-14	1 Corinthians 1.3-9	1 Thessalonians 3.9-13
Matthew 24.36-44	Mark 13.24-37	Luke 21.25-36

The Second Sunday in Advent

Year A	Year B	Year C
Isaiah 11.1-10	Isaiah 40.1-11	Baruch 5.1-9
Romans 15.4-13	2 Peter 3.8-15a	Philippians 1.3-11
Matthew 3.1-12	Mark 1.1-8	Luke 3.1-6

The Third Sunday in Advent

Year A	Year B	Year C
Isaiah 35.1-10	Isaiah 61.1-4, 8-11	Zephaniah 3.14-20
James 5.7-10	1 Thessalonians 5.16-24	Philippians 4.4-7
Matthew 11.2-11	John 1.6-8,19-28	Luke 3.7-18

The Fourth Sunday in Advent

YEAR A	YEAR B	YEAR C
Isaiah 7.10-16	2 Samuel 7.10,11,16	Micah 5.2-5a
Romans 1.1-7	Romans 16.25-27	Hebrews 10.5-10
Matthew 1.18-25	Luke 1.26-38	Luke 1.39-45

Prayer

The First Sunday of Advent

Almighty God,
give us grace to cast away the works of darkness
and to put on the armour of light,
now in the time of this mortal life,
in which your Son Jesus Christ
    came to us in great humility;
that on the last day,
when he shall come again in his glorious majesty
    to judge the living and the dead,
we may rise to the life immortal;
through him who is alive and reigns with you,
in the unity of the Holy Spirit,
one God, now and for ever. Amen.

The Second Sunday of Advent

O Lord, raise up, we pray, your power
and come among us,
and with great might succour us;
that whereas, through our sins and wickedness
we are grievously hindered
in running the race that is set before us,
your bountiful grace and mercy
may speedily help and deliver us;
through Jesus Christ your Son our Lord,
to whom with you and the Holy Spirit
be honour and glory, now and for ever. Amen.

The Third Sunday of Advent

O Lord Jesus Christ,
who at your first coming sent your messenger
to prepare your way before you:
grant that the ministers and stewards of your
    mysteries
may likewise so prepare and make ready your way
by turning the hearts of the disobedient
    to the wisdom of the just,
that at your second coming to judge the world
we may be found an acceptable people in your
    sight;
for your are alive and reign with the Father
in the unity of the Holy Spirit,
one God, now and for ever. Amen.

The Fourth Sunday of Advent

God, our redeemer,
who prepared the Blessed Virgin Mary
to be the mother of your Son:
grant that, as she looked for his coming as our
    saviour,
so we may be ready to greet him
when he comes again as our judge;
who is alive and reigns with you,
in the unity of the Holy Spirit,
one God, now and for ever. Amen.

(all from *Common Worship*)

Grace before a meal

We thank you, Father, maker of heaven and earth,
for the food and shelter of this home,
for the hope you give us in the scriptures,
And for the light you bring us in Jesus Christ. Amen.

(*The Promise of His Glory*, p. 143)

Preparing the home

The Jesse Tree

Prince Albert brought the custom of the Christmas tree from Germany during Victorian times. The Jesse Tree is used to depict the ancestors of Jesus, and can be seen in stained-glass windows in medieval churches and cathedrals. Jesse was the father of King David, the ancestor of Jesus: 'A shoot shall sprout from the stump of Jesse and from his roots a bud shall blossom' (Isaiah 11.7).

A Jesse Tree can be made from a bare branch sprayed white or gold and set in an empty vase or pot, or you could use a Christmas tree instead. The tree is decorated with symbols that trace ancestors and events in the Bible from Creation through to the Nativity. Below is a list of symbols that can be used for a Jesse Tree. You could try making just a few to begin with and then adding to them year by year. If you make the symbols from card these can be decorated with foil, glitter, etc.

In our family we place a symbol on the tree each evening throughout Advent. We read the Bible story first and then hang the symbol on the tree starting with the bottom branches and working to the top.

Symbols for an Advent Jesse Tree

Bible story	Bible reference		Symbols
Creation	Genesis	1.1-2.2	World; sun; stars; animals; plants; birds, etc.
Fall and promise	Genesis	3.1-15	Tree with fruit; serpent; angel with sword
Noah	Genesis	6.9-22	Ark; waves; olive branch; pairs of animals
		7.17-19	Waves
		8.6-22	Dove; olive branch
		9.8-17	Rainbow
Abraham	Genesis	12.1-5	Shepherd's crook
		13.14-18	Oak tree
Isaac	Genesis	22.1-19	Donkey; bundles of sticks; knife; altar with fire; ram; sand; stars
Jacob	Genesis	28.10-18	Ladder; angel; stone
Joseph	Genesis	37.2-36	Coloured coat; sheaf of wheat; pyramid

Symbols for an Advent Jesse Tree (contd)

Moses	Exodus	2.1-10	Basket
		3.1-12	Burning bush
		12.1-20	Passover lamb; bread
		14.15-31	Paths through waters
		16.1-16	Manna; quails
		20	Commandments on stone tablets
Joshua	Joshua	6.1-21	Trumpets
Ruth	Ruth	1.1-22	Sheaf of wheat
David	1 Samuel	16.1-13	Horn of oil
	1 Samuel	17.40-52	Sling
	1 Samuel	18.10	Harp
	2 Samuel	7.8-16	Crown; six-pointed star
Solomon	1 Kings	3.4-15	Heart
		8.1-7	Art
		8.10-19	Temple
Judith	Judith	9,10,11	Mirror, knife
Isaiah	Isaiah	1.1-6	Scroll
		16-20	Red and white wool
Jeremiah	Jeremiah	1.1-10	Hand touching mouth
		31.31-34	Love
Ezekiel	Ezekiel	11.17-21	Heart
Daniel	Daniel	3.19-25	Three men in fire
		6.11-28	A man; lion

Coming of Jesus

Trinity	Romans	5.1-5	Triangle
Holy Spirit	1 Corinthians	12.3-7,12-13	Dove
Gabriel	Luke	1.11,19,26-29	Angel; trumpet
Zechariah	Luke	1.5-25,57-66	Smoking incense; sealed lips
Elizabeth	Luke	1.39-45	Old woman with baby
John the Baptist	Matthew	11.7-15	Desert; locusts; honey
Joseph	Matthew	1.18-25	Carpenter's tools
Mary	Mark	3.31-35	Young woman with baby
	Luke	8.19-21	'M'
Jesus	Luke	1.31-33	Candle or lamp
		2.1-7	Crib or manger; cross
Shepherds	Luke	2.8-20	Shepherd's staff; lamb
Wise Men	Matthew	2.1-12	Gifts; star; camel
Simeon and Anna	Luke	2.22-38	Old couple; our faith journey leading up to Jesus' birth

8

The crib

The first Christmas crib is attributed to St Francis of Assisi and was created in the year 1223. He had made a wooden manger that he surrounded with live animals on Christmas Eve. People from the town visited the crib, where they heard the story of Jesus and sang carols in praise of his birth. It was intended as a way to teach people about the birth of Jesus and as an object of decoration. There is an element of penitence at the crib as we respond to the God who loves us and calls us by name.

Most churches and cathedrals use a crib during the season of Christmas, but it is also a lovely thing to do in the home as well. If you don't own a crib set they can be bought inexpensively. Alternatively, you can make your own unique crib using pipe-cleaners and scraps of material. The crib could be set up on Christmas Eve or begun a few days earlier, adding one character each evening. Finish off by putting the Christ child in after the service on Christmas Eve or on Christmas morning. The wise men can travel towards the crib for the next twelve days along the mantel-shelf, across book cases and over the sideboard, following the star.

Blessing of the crib

When you have finished arranging the crib and figures, you may wish to use the following prayers:

Leader:	Bless, O Lord, this crib.
	May it remind us of the first Christmas.
All:	**Blessed be God forever.**
Leader:	Let us rejoice at the birth of your Son in the world.
All:	**Blessed be God forever.**
Leader:	Prepare each of us to receive you and walk in ways of justice and peace.
All:	**Blessed be God forever.**

The verses of this, or another carol can be sung:

1. O little town of Bethlehem,
   how still we see you lie!
   Above your deep and dreamless sleep
   the silent stars go by:
   yet in your dark streets shining
   is everlasting light;
   the hopes and fears of all the years
   are met in you tonight.

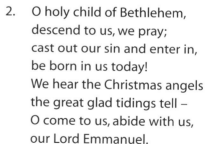

2. O holy child of Bethlehem,
   descend to us, we pray;
   cast out our sin and enter in,
   be born in us today!
   We hear the Christmas angels
   the great glad tidings tell –
   O come to us, abide with us,
   our Lord Emmanuel.

   (P. Brooks, 1835–93)

 # Activities

Advent wreath

Use an Advent wreath as you count down to Christmas Day. You will need:

a dish

florist's foam well soaked in water

five candles:

three purple or red – week 1 for the patriarchs, week 2 for the prophets, week 3 for John the Baptist,

one pink – for Mary, lit on the fourth Sunday,

one white – for Christ, lit on Christmas Day,

and evergreen foliage.

Start by cutting the florist's foam to fit the dish. Push the candles into the foam. The white candle should be placed in the middle and the three purple (or red) and one pink one placed around the edge, spaced at intervals. Then proceed to cover and fill the foam with evergreens, starting from the outer edge and then working in towards the middle.

The following prayers can be said at the lighting of candles, or you may wish to sing the Advent Wreath Song (see page 11).

First Sunday in Advent

Lord Jesus, Light of the world,
Born in David's city of Bethlehem,
Born like him to be a king:
Be born in our hearts this Christmastide,
Be king of our lives today. Amen.

Second Sunday in Advent

Lord Jesus, Light of the world,
The prophets said you would bring peace
And save your people in trouble.
Give peace in our hearts at Christmastide,
And show all the world God's love. Amen.

Third Sunday in Advent

Lord Jesus, light of the world,
John told the people to prepare,
For you were very near.
As Christmas grows closer day by day,
Help us to be ready to welcome you now. Amen.

Fourth Sunday in Advent

Lord Jesus, Light of the world,
Blessed is Gabriel who brought good news;
Blessed is Mary your mother and ours.
Bless your Church preparing for Christmas;
and bless us your children who long for your
    coming. Amen.

Christmas Day

Lord Jesus, Light of Light,
you have come among us.
Help us to live by your light
to shine as lights in your world.
Glory to God in the highest! Amen.

(all from *The Promise of His Glory*, pp. 137-40)

Advent Wreath Song

This is sung to the tune of 'The Holly and the Ivy'. Each week, as Advent progresses and the next candle is lit, we sing an additional verse from the following song.

Advent 1

1. The holly and the ivy
   Are dancing in a ring
   Round the berry bright red candles
   And the white and shining king.

2. Oh, one is for the patriarchs
   Who heard and lived your call.
   They brought us to your promised land,
   Bringing hope, that none may fall.

Advent 2

3. Oh, two is for the prophets
   And for the light they bring
   They are candles in the darkness,
   All alight for Christ the king.

Advent 3

4. And three is John the Baptist.
   He calls on us to sing:
   'Oh prepare the way for Jesus Christ,
   He is coming, Christ the king'.

Advent 4

5. And four for mother Mary,
   'I cannot see the way,
   But you promise me a baby
   I believe you, I obey'.

And on Christmas Day

6. And Christ is in the centre,
   For this is his birthday,
   With shining lights of Christmas
   Singing: 'He has come today'.

'O' antiphon decorations

The Advent antiphons are used before and after the Magnificat at Evening Prayer between 17th and 23rd December. They are sentences which explain the different characteristics attributed to Jesus Christ. When used during the week before Christmas, they can intensify the sense of expectation and preparation. They help us to look, not at what God has done for us in the past, but what he will do for us in the future. They proclaim future hope and judgement.

An antiphon poster can be made for each day and displayed in the home. Our children create posters in the early weeks of Advent to be used during the last few days, with the appropriate prayers and readings.

The dates, titles and symbols for the 'O' antiphons are printed on page 12. You could try using as many different art mediums as you can, for example paint, pastels, collage, glitter and foil, to create the effect you desire or make your image in three dimensions, as we did, when making the crown for 'O king of the nations'.

Find an appropriate place to display these posters – we placed ours on the walls of the staircase and the upstairs landing. This made an appropriate place to stand or sit as we listened to the readings and joined in the responses at the children's bedtime. Alternatively, the posters can be placed along a wall leading to the place where the crib has been arranged. It also gives opportunities during the day to stop, pause and reflect on your Advent preparations as you go about the house.

Date	Antiphon	Symbol
17th December	O wisdom	A two-edged sword
18th December	O Lord of lords	A burning bush or the earth with God's hands around it
19th December	O root of Jesse	A flowering tree or branch
20th December	O key of David	A key
21st December	O morning star	A rising sun
22nd December	O king of the nations	A crown
23rd December	O Emmanuel	Crib in a stable

17th December

Leader: O wisdom, coming forth from the Most High, filling all creation and reigning to the ends of the earth; come and teach us the way of truth.

All: **Amen. Come, Lord Jesus.**

Reading: *Ecclesiasticus 24.3-9* [from the Apocrypha].

To be sung or said:

> Oh come, thou wisdom from on high
> who madest all in earth and sky,
> creating man from dust and clay:
> to us reveal salvation's way.

All sing: **Rejoice! Rejoice! Emmanuel shall come to thee, O Israel.**

18th December

Leader: O Lord of Lords, and ruler of the House of Israel, you appeared to Moses in the fire of burning bush, and gave him the law on Sinai: come with your outstretched arm and ransom us.

All: **Amen. Come, Lord Jesus.**

Reading: *Exodus 3.1-6.*

To be sung or said:

> O come, O come, Adonai,
> who in thy glorious majesty
> from Sinai's mountain, clothed in awe,
> gavest thy folk the ancient law.

All sing: **Rejoice! Rejoice! Emmanuel shall come to thee, O Israel.**

19th December

Leader: O root of Jesse, standing as a sign among the nations; kings will keep silence before you for whom the nations long; come and save us and delay no longer.

All: **Amen. Come, Lord Jesus.**

Reading: *Isaiah 11.1-4a.*

To be sung or said:

> O come, thou root of Jesse! Draw
> the quarry from the lion's claw;
> from those dread caverns of the grave, from nether hell thy people save.

All sing: **Rejoice! Rejoice! Emmanuel shall come to thee, O Israel.**

20th December

Leader: O key of David and sceptre of the house of Israel; you open and none can shut; you shut and none can open: come and free the captives from prison, and break down the walls of death.

All: **Amen. Come, Lord Jesus.**

Reading: *Isaiah 22.21-23.*

To be sung or said:

O come, thou Lord of David's key! The royal door fling wide and free; safeguard for us the heavenward road, and bar the way to death's abode.

All sing: **Rejoice! Rejoice! Emmanuel shall come to thee, O Israel.**

21st December

Leader: O morning star, splendour of the light eternal and bright sun of right-eousness: come and bring light to those who dwell in darkness and walk in the shadow of death.

All: **Amen. Come, Lord Jesus.**

Reading: *Numbers 24.15b-17.*

To be sung or said:

Oh come, O come, thou dayspring bright!
Pour on our souls thy healing light; dispel the long night's lingering gloom,
and pierce the shadows of the tomb.

All sing: **Rejoice! Rejoice! Emmanuel shall come to thee, O Israel.**

22nd December

Leader: O king of the nations, you alone can fulfil their desires: cornerstone, bind-ing all together: come and save the creature you fashioned from the dust of the earth.

All: **Amen. Come, Lord Jesus.**

Reading: *Jeremiah 30.7-11a.*

To be sung or said:

O come, desire of nations! Show thy kingly reign on earth below; thou cornerstone, uniting all, restore the ruin of our fall.

All sing: **Rejoice! Rejoice! Emmanuel shall come to thee, O Israel.**

23rd December

Leader: O Emmanuel our King and Lawgiver, hope of the nations and their saviour: come and save us, O Lord our God.

All: **Amen. Come, Lord Jesus.**

The Gospel reading: *Matthew 1.18-23.*

Leader: A reading from the Holy Gospel according to Matthew.

All: **Glory to Christ our Saviour.**

At the end the reader says:

This is the gospel of Christ.

All: **Praise to Christ our Lord.**

To be sung or said:

O come, O come, Emmanuel!
Redeem thy captive Israel,
that into exile drear is gone
far from the face of God's dear Son.

All sing: **Rejoice! Rejoice! Emmanuel shall come to thee, O Israel.**

(all from *The Promise of His Glory*, pp. 114–16)

Thoughts for food

'O' antiphon ring

To mark the last remaining days of Advent and to increase the anticipation for Christmas, the Church has traditionally used the 'O' antiphons in its liturgy. They are known as the 'O' antiphons because they begin 'O' rod of Jesse, 'O' key of David, 'O' king of kings, and so forth. They are rich in symbolism and you could use these symbols too in your preparations by making a simple pas-try dish to cut and share on each day.

You will need (approximately):

450–475 g (1–1½ lb) puff pastry (depending on the number of people in your family)

450 g (1 lb) mincemeat

450 g (1 lb) Cox's eating apples, cored and sliced icing sugar and water to make a glacé icing (optional)

packets of ready-rolled icing in various colours (optional)

1. Roll out the puff pastry into a long thin oblong shape.
2. Spread the mincemeat along one half, lengthways, and cover with sliced apples. Wet the edge and fold over, then press down to seal.
3. Place the pastry roll on a baking tray and form into a ring shape. Then seal the ends together.
4. Bake at 220°C (425°F or gas mark 7) for approximately 20–30 minutes until puffed and golden.
5. When the pastry ring is cool you can cover with glacé icing.
6. Use the ready-roll icing to make symbols for each of the antiphons. Divide the ring into seven equal portions, making a mark in the

glacé icing, then place a symbol on each portion. Cut and slice each of the portions on the appropriate day for that antiphon. Store the ring in the fridge to keep it fresh.

The following are suggestions for the symbols you might make in fondant icing:

O wisdom	A sword
O Lord of lords	The earth held by hands
O root of Jesse	A tree
O key of David	A key
O morning star	The sun
O king of the nations	A crown
O Emmanuel	A manger

Alternatively, you could draw the symbols on paper and stick them onto the ring with icing sugar.

Biscuits for St Nicholas

The feast of St Nicholas is kept on 6th December. In many parts of Europe, for example Germany, Holland and Austria, St Nicholas does not visit children's homes on Christmas Eve, but on his feast day, 6th December. He is not dressed in a red coat, fur trimmed hood and boots, but in his bishop's robes.

St Nicholas was a bishop in the fourth century at a place called Myra in Asia Minor. He is the patron saint of children, sailors and pawnbrokers. Legend says that he helped three girls to get married by providing dowries of three bags of gold for them.

Spicy biscuits are traditionally eaten on St Nicholas' Day and the following recipe may be used. In our family we always make a large biscuit in the shape of St Nicholas as a bishop.

You will need:

> 400 g (14 oz) plain flour
> 3 level tsp baking powder
> 350 g (12 oz) granulated sugar
> 2 medium eggs
> 6 tbsp milk
> a pinch each of ginger, ground cloves, nutmeg and white pepper
> 1 tsp cinnamon
> 25 g (1 oz) ground almonds
> 15 g (½ oz) candied lemon, diced very small

1. Mix the flour and baking powder and sieve onto a board.
2. Make a hollow in the middle, add the eggs, sugar, milk, and spices and work in part of the flour using a fork.
3. Add the rest of the ingredients and knead to a smooth dough.
4. Roll out to 1 cm thick and cut out round biscuit shapes – or you can use the template for St Nicholas to make one large biscuit and decorate with coloured icing when cooked.
5. Cook at 175°C (350°F, gas mark 4) for about 20 minutes.

St Lucia, 13th December

St Lucia's Day on 13th December is another winter festival of lights and candles. It is celebrated particularly in Sweden and is becoming better known in the rest of Europe too.

Here in Britain, at the Swedish Church in London, St Lucia is celebrated every year. You can obtain tickets from the church (it is so popular that it takes place over two or three days) and take part in the worship and songs.

St Lucia was a young Sicilian girl who died for her Christian beliefs in the fourth century. Her name means 'light'. In Sweden a young girl dressed in white with a crown of candles brings coffee and cake to members of her family as they wake in the morning.

Here is a recipe for saffron buns, which are traditionally brought by St Lucia.

For about 30 saffron buns you will need:

> 2 tsp saffron powder
> 25 g (1 oz) yeast (or 2 packets active dry yeast)
> 600 ml (1 pint) milk
> 175 g (6 oz) butter
> ½ tsp salt
> 175 g (6 oz) caster sugar
> 1 medium egg
> 800 g (1¾ lb) plain flour
> 50 g (2 oz) chopped almonds
> 90 g (3½ oz) raisins
> 65 g (2½ oz) chopped mixed peel

1. Place the yeast in a mixing bowl and cream with a few tablespoons of the milk.
2. Melt the butter in a saucepan. Pour the rest of the milk onto the butter and warm until tepid. Then add the saffron.
3. Pour the warm milk mixture onto the yeast and stir in the salt, sugar, half the flour, the egg, almonds, raisins and mixed peel.
4. Add the remaining flour and knead the dough for about 5 minutes, until smooth. Cover with a damp cloth and leave in a warm place to rise until doubled in size.
5. Knead the dough again on a floured surface, then divide it into 30 buns and place on a greased baking tray.
6. Bake at 210°C (425°F, gas mark 7) for approximately 10–15 minutes.

Food for thought

✦ In what ways can we, as a family, make Jesus known in our lives? What part of the community in which you live needs the presence of Jesus?

✦ If you were to organize a surprise birthday party for Jesus, who would you invite and what presents would you buy?

✦ What is the best thing that God has ever given you?

Christmas

Background

The traditional twelve days of Christmas begin on Christmas Day and last until 5th January, the day before the Epiphany is celebrated. This period of twelve days is called Christmastide. At its heart is the celebration of the birth of Christ on Christmas Day. It is God being born in human form, incarnate in the world, light coming into darkness. It is a time of praise and thanksgiving.

After the anticipation and build-up of Advent, Christmas finally arrives. In our family we have the tradition of attending Midnight Mass. On our return home we place the figure of the Baby Jesus in the Christmas Crib with a final prayer before going to bed.

During the Christmas season we try to spend time with family and friends, enjoying each other's company and taking part in the usual Christmas fun. We often act out a very simple mummer's play for which we all enjoy making the props and costumes.

Bible readings

Isaiah 52.7-10
Hebrews 1.1-4
John 1.1-14

Prayer

Almighty God,
you have given us your only-begotten Son
to take our nature upon him
and as at this time to be born of a pure virgin:
grant that we, who have been born again
and made your children by adoption and grace,
may daily be renewed by your Holy Spirit;
through Jesus Christ your Son our Lord,
who is alive and reigns with you,
in the unity of the Holy Spirit,
one God, now and for ever. Amen.

(Collect for Christmas Day from *Common Worship*)

Grace before a meal

We thank you, Father, giver of all good things,
for the joy of the season of Christmas,
for the good news of a Saviour,
and for the wonder of the Word made flesh,
your Son, Jesus Christ, our Lord. Amen.

(*The Promise of His Glory*, p. 143)

Activity

Mummers' play

Mummers' plays are some of England's oldest Christmas traditions. In the plays, people dressed

up and acted out the fight between darkness and light. Here is a short play that contains the traditional characters. You may wish to write your own.

Cast:

Bold Knight, dressed in black
Sir George, dressed in white
Doctor, dressed in green
Father Christmas, dressed in red and white
Little Jack, dressed in any colour

Little Jack: In come I, little Johnny Jack, I see the winter has come back,
But rain or snow won't keep me away,
I've come to see your mummers' play.
Ladies and gentlemen, give what you please,
Give it to old Father Chrissymas, please.

Father Christmas:

In come I, Old Father Christmas,
Welcome or welcome not,
I hope old Father Christmas
Will never be forgot!
Although we've got but a short time to stay,
We've come to show you a jolly old play.
In comes our hero dressed in white,
He's bold Sir George, yes, George the knight.

Sir George: In come I, St George the bold,
Oh, I say, this country's cold.
I've been away to warmer lands,
Fighting a dragon with my hands.
I at last brought him to slaughter
And now I'll marry the king's fair daughter.

Bold Knight: In come I, the big, bold Knight,
I've nothing to do so I fancied a fight.
I'll fight St George, he's supposed to be strong,
But between you and me, he won't live long!

(St George and the Bold Knight take out wooden swords and fight. The Bold Knight wins. St George falls to the ground. The audience shouts out 'Aaaah!'.)

Doctor: In come I, the good Doctor Chubb,
I'll wake Sir George with my strong club.

(Pretends to bash George with the mallet, but actually hits the floor to make a loud thud.)

I'll sprinkle him with lots of water
To make him fit for the king's dear daughter.
I'll put some powder on his head,
Rise up, Sir George, you're no longer dead.

(Cheers from the audience.)

Father Christmas and Little Jack:

Hurray! Hurray! Our play is done,
Bold Knight has lost, Sir George has won,
We can no longer wait around here,
Merry Christmas and a happy New Year.

Thoughts for food

Candied sweet potatoes

You could try these with the turkey. You will need:

6 medium-sized sweet potatoes
100 g (4 oz) brown sugar
25 g (1 oz) butter or margarine,
½ tsp grated lime peel
a pinch of ground ginger
½ tsp salt

1. Wash the potatoes and place them in a saucepan with boiling water to cover. Cover the pan and cook over a moderate heat for about 30 minutes, or until the potatoes are just tender. Drain them and allow them to cool, then peel.

2. Preheat the oven to 190°C (375°F, gas mark 5) while the potatoes are cooling.

3. Cut the potatoes into halves lengthways, and place them in a shallow baking dish.
4. Heat the sugar, butter, lime peel, ginger and salt in a small saucepan over moderate heat until the butter and sugar have melted. Then pour this mixture over the potatoes.
5. Bake uncovered for 20–25 minutes, basting occasionally with the sauce to glaze the potatoes.

Phulowrie

These are good for parties. You will need:

450 g (1 lb) split peas
2 cloves garlic, crushed
1 tsp saffron powder
¼ tsp bicarbonate of soda
2 tsp baking powder
2 tbsp flour
1½ tsp salt
1 tsp tabasco sauce

1. Wash the split peas and soak them overnight.
2. Next day, drain them and grind in a food processor or food mill, until the consistency is smooth. Add the garlic, saffron powder, bicarbonate of soda, baking powder, flour, salt and tabasco, and allow to rest for one hour. If the mixture seems too dry add a little water.
3. Beat the mixture with a wooden spoon: this incorporates air to lighten the mixture.
4. Heat oil in a deep fryer, and drop teaspoonfuls of the phulowrie mixture into the hot oil. Fry until golden brown or until the phulowrie float to the top of the oil.
5. Drain and serve immediately with chutney.

Pumpkin accras

You will need:

100 g (4 oz) grated pumpkin
1 medium egg
50 g (2 oz) flour
½ tsp baking powder

1 tsp ground black pepper
2 tbsp freshly chopped spring onion
1 tsp salt
oil for frying

1. Combine all the ingredients.
2. Heat the oil in a frying pan and drop tablespoonfuls of the mixture into the hot oil.
3. Turn over when cooked on one side.
4. When cooked on both sides, remove and drain on kitchen paper. Serve while still hot.

Rum punch

This is guaranteed to make your Christmas go with a swing! You will need:

125 ml (4 fl oz) lime juice (freshly squeezed)
225 g (8 oz) sugar
350 ml (12 fl oz) rum
425 ml (16 fl oz) water
spices to taste – cloves, cinnamon, nutmeg, etc.

Mix all the ingredients together and bottle.

(Recipe of the late Mrs Enid Coo)

Food for thought

Read the Nativity story again.

✦ Ask each member of the family which character in the story they identify with and why?

✦ What is the greatest gift anyone could give to God?

✦ Think about the qualities and skills that make you unique. In what ways are you a gift to God?

Epiphany

Colour: gold or white

Background

The Feast of the Epiphany falls on 6th January. It is the final day of the twelve days that mark the Christmas season, and so it is named Twelfth Night.

On this day the Church celebrates the time when Jesus was made known to the wider world, the time when the wise men, Caspar, Melchior and Balthazar, came to worship him, and invited all of us to do the same. They returned to share what they had seen and heard with others. Epiphany reminds us of our own mission to make known the story of God's love with those around us.

There is a tradition of baking a cake for this day, into which has been placed a large coin. Whoever finds this in their slice of cake is 'King ' or 'Queen' for the remainder of the day.

In some countries the Feast of the Epiphany is the day when gifts are given. It is a day of celebration that lends itself to a party. It is traditionally the day when all Christmas decorations are taken down.

On the feast of the Epiphany, as we take the Christmas decorations down we leave the crib up for a week longer and the wise men who have been making their slow progress across the hearth and up and across the bookcase finally make their arrival at the crib. This day also marks the departure of the shepherds.

As we take down our Christmas decorations at tea-time we usually eat star-shaped sandwiches and star-shaped shortbread biscuits. We also like to keep back a Christmas gift for this moment, to remember the gifts the kings brought to the infant Jesus. Sometimes we invite family and friends to an Epiphany party and ideas for this can be found in this chapter.

Bible readings

Isaiah 60.1-6
Ephesians 3.1-12
Matthew 2.1-12

Prayer

O God
who by the leading of a star
manifested your only Son to the peoples of the earth:
mercifully grant that we,
who know you now by faith,
may at last behold your glory face to face;
through Jesus Christ your Son our Lord,
who is alive and reigns with you,
in the unity of the Holy Spirit,
one God, now and for ever. Amen.

(Collect for Epiphany from *Common Worship*)

Grace before a meal

We thank you, Father, God of love,
for the signs of your love on this table,
for your love made known through all the world
and shining on us in the face of Jesus Christ,
  our Lord. Amen.

(*The Promise of His Glory*, p. 143)

Preparing the home

The Feast of the Epiphany is the day when the three kings or wise men arrived at the Christmas crib. There are many legends surrounding the three visitors to the stable. Tradition has it that they were three kings – Melchior, an old man with grey hair and beard, was King of Arabia and brought the gift of gold, Caspar, a young and beardless man, was King of Sheba and brought the gift of frankincense, and Balthazar, with black hair and beard, was King of Egypt and Tarse, and brought the gift of myrrh.

The gifts all have a special meaning: gold is seen as the most precious metal, fit for the king, Jesus; frankincense (incense) was used in temple worship and is still burnt in some churches today as a sign of God's presence; myrrh is a fragrant spice that was used to prepare bodies for burial, and reminds us of the suffering and death Jesus was to undergo.

The following may be helpful to guide the kings on their way:

Three volunteers are needed to be Caspar, Balthazar and Melchior. Each holds their crib figure and joins in the singing or saying of 'We three kings' as they place them in the crib:

All: We three kings of Orient are;
bearing gifts we traverse afar;
field and fountain,
moor and mountain,
following yonder star.

All: *(Chorus)*
O star of wonder, star of night,
star with royal beauty bright;
westward leading, still proceeding,
guide us to thy perfect light.

Melchior: Born a king on Bethlehem plain,
gold I bring to crown him again,
king for ever, ceasing never
over us all to reign.

All: *Chorus*

Caspar: Frankincense to offer have I,
incense owns a Deity nigh,
prayer and praising gladly raising,
worship him, God most high.

All: *Chorus*

Balthazar: Myrrh is mine, its bitter perfume
breathes a life of gathering gloom;
sorrowing, sighing, bleeding, dying,
sealed in the stone-cold tomb.

All: *Chorus*

All: Glorious now, behold him arise,
King and God and sacrifice;
alleluia, alleluia,
earth to heav'n replies.

(J. H. Hopkins, 1820-91)

Reading: *Matthew 2.1-12*

Reader 1:   Lord, we search for you. We bring our gift of gold and name you king of kings.

All: **May we see you Lord.**

Reader 1:   Lord, we long for you. We bring our gift of frankincense and name you Lord of lords.

All: **May we see you Lord.**

Reader 1:   Lord, we hope for you. We bring our gift of myrrh and name you servant of us all.

All: **May we see you Lord.**

(A candle may be lit.)

Reader 2:   The wise men followed the star, and found Christ who is the light of the world. May we find Christ and walk in his light.

Let us say the grace together:

The grace of our Lord, Jesus Christ,
and the love of God,
and the fellowship of the Holy Spirit,
be with us all, evermore. Amen.

 # Activities
Follow that star!

We can journey with the wise men to Bethlehem by making an Epiphany board game. Number each consecutive square on a large piece of card. Here are some suggestions which you might include that help or hinder the wise men on their journey.

1. You see the star – go forward five spaces.
2. You hear the voice of Herod – miss a turn.
3. You are refreshed at an oasis – go forward two spaces.
4. A rock fall bars your way – go back three spaces.
5. A sand storm blows up – miss a turn.
6. You find a short cut – go forward three spaces.
7. You see a signpost 'to Bethlehem' – go forward four spaces.

You may also want to include some Bible references, so if you land on one of those squares you have to read the reference out. You might include some or all of the following:

1. John 4.7-26
2. Isaiah 60.1-6
3. Matthew 2.1-12
4. Ephesians 3.1-12
5. Jeremiah 31.7-14
6. John 1.29-34.

You will also need counters and a dice to play the game.

Epiphany party

You might like to celebrate Epiphany with a party. You could make star-shaped sandwiches and biscuits or decorate a cake with a star. The star theme could lend itself to the decorations you might like to put up or leave up when the Christmas decorations come down. A game of 'pass the parcel' would be appropriate for the season of Epiphany. You might like to keep one Christmas gift back to be opened at the Epiphany party.

Thoughts for food
Epiphany surprise

You will need:

450 g (1 lb) wholemeal plain flour
2 tsp mixed spice
1 tsp bicarbonate of soda
170 g (6 oz) butter or margarine, chilled and diced
230 g (8 oz) soft, dark brown sugar
230 g (8 oz) sultanas
1 medium egg, beaten

280 ml (½ pint) cider
85 ml (3 fl oz) milk
10 demerara sugar cubes
20.5 cm (8 in) square cake tin, greased and lined, and one large scrubbed coin

1. Set the oven at 170°C (325°F, gas mark 3).
2. Mix the flour with the mixed spice and bicarbonate of soda.
3. Rub in the fat until the mixture resembles fine breadcrumbs, then stir in the sugar and sultanas.
4. Mix the egg with the cider and milk, then stir thoroughly into the flour mixture, and add the coin.
5. Spoon the mixture into the prepared tin.
6. Finally, lightly crush the sugar cubes using a rolling pin, and sprinkle over the cake.
7. Bake for 1½ –1¾ hours, or until a skewer inserted into the centre comes out clean. Turn out and cool on a wire rack.

The cake can be decorated with a crown made from a gold-coloured piece of card or paper.

Candlemas

Colour: gold or white

Background

Candlemas, or the Feast of the Presentation of our Lord in the Temple, falls on 2nd February. This day celebrates the event of Jesus being taken by his parents to the Temple in Jerusalem where they offered thanks. It was in the Temple that Simeon, with his wife Anna, recognized Jesus as the expected one, the Messiah. Simeon said that Jesus would be a light to all people. It is for this reason that candles are used in the church worship. Candlemas marks a pivotal point where we look back to the Christmas period and forward to the events of Jesus' Passion.

It was the Jewish custom at the time of Jesus that every first-born son must be offered to God in the Temple on the eighth day after his birth. The mother also had to follow custom by offering the appropriate sacrifice in order to be ritually cleansed.

When Jesus was offered to God in the Temple, Simeon and Anna recognized that all God's people were purified and brought back into a right relationship with God because of Jesus' presence among them.

At home we light lots of candles for the evening meal in a darkened room and we remind the children what a difference even one candle can make in the dark.

Bible readings

Malachi 3.1-5
Hebrews 2.14-18
Luke 2.22-40

Prayers

Nunc Dimittis

Lord now you let your servant go in peace:
your word has been fulfilled.
My own eyes have seen the salvation:
which you have prepared in the sight of
  every people.
A light to reveal you to the nations:
and the glory of your people Israel.
Glory to the Father, and to the Son,
and to the Holy Spirit:
as it was in the beginning, is now,
and shall be for ever. Amen.

(The Promise of His Glory, pp. 280–81)

Almighty and ever-living God,
clothed in majesty,
whose beloved Son
  was this day presented in the Temple,
in substance of our flesh:
grant that we may be presented to you
with pure and clean hearts,
by your Son Jesus Christ our Lord,
who is alive and reigns with you,
in the unity of the Holy Spirit,
one God, now and for ever. Amen.

(Collect for the Presentation of Christ in the Temple
from *Common Worship*)

Grace before a meal

We thank you Father, light of all nations,
for your love reflected in this meal.
May our lives reflect your love to those we
  meet,
through Jesus Christ our Lord. Amen.

Activity

Candlemas lantern

To make a Candlemas lantern you will need a plain glass tumbler or a jam jar large enough to fit a night light in the bottom. You will also need glass paints, which you can obtain from craft shops. Following the instructions for using glass paints you can decorate the glass with symbols of faith.

Our children's favourites have been: flames, to represent the light of Christ or the Holy Spirit; a cross, to represent the love of Jesus; and a heart, to represent God's love. We then place the finished lantern on the table at meals or use it at prayer times.

Thoughts for food

Candlemas biscuits

You will need:

175 g (6 oz) butter or margarine
50 g (2 oz) caster sugar
225 g (8 oz) plain flour
2 level dessertspoons of ground rice
coloured icing for decoration
cardboard for template

1. Draw and cut out a candle with a flame from the card and use it as a template for the biscuits.
2. Cream the butter or margarine and sugar and add the flour and ground rice.
3. Knead into a dough and then roll out onto a floured board to about 5 mm thick.
4. Cut into candle shapes and put them onto a baking tin about 4 cm apart.
5. Cook at 190°C (375°F, gas mark 5) for about 20 minutes.
6. Once cool, decorate with icing sugar with the names of those whose lives reflect God's love.

Food for thought

✦ If you could see God, what do you think he would look like?

✦ Remember a time when you felt God was close to you. What was that time and were there other people with you? What were your thoughts and feelings at the time?

✦ Light a candle and look at the flame. Describe the character and qualities of the flame. How is God like the flame? What do we mean when we say Christ is the light of the world?

Ash Wednesday
The first day of Lent

Background

Ash Wednesday marks the first day of the penitential season of Lent. The palm crosses that were given out at the previous year's Palm Sunday will have been collected and burnt. The ash remaining is used by the priest to mark on each person's forehead the sign of the cross with the words 'Remember that thou art dust, and to dust thou shalt return. Repent and believe the gospel'. It is traditionally a day of fasting.

Preparing the home
Lenten cross

You will need:

- 4 purple candles
- 1 pink candle
- 1 white candle
- two pieces of wood at least 3 cm thick

Wood can be saved from a Christmas tree, which symbolizes the journey with Christ from his birth to death and resurrection.

Join the two pieces by cutting out the wood and drilling holes wide enough to accept the candles, as shown. The white candle placed in the centre of the cross is to be lit on Easter Day, and the pink candle on Refreshment or Mothering Sunday, which falls on the fourth Sunday in Lent. The other candles are to be lit in turn, beginning with the first Sunday in Lent. This can be placed on the meal table or in a prominent position in the home.

Bible readings

Isaiah 58.1-12
2 Corinthians 5.20b–6.10
John 8.1-11

Prayer

Almighty and everlasting God,
you hate nothing that you have made
and forgive the sins of all those who are
   penitent:
create and make in us new and contrite hearts
that we, worthily lamenting our sins
and acknowledging our wretchedness,
may receive from you, the God of all mercy,
perfect remission and forgiveness;
through Jesus Christ your Son our Lord,
who is alive and reigns with you,
in the unity of the Holy Spirit,
one God, now and for ever. Amen.

(Collect for Ash Wednesday from *Common Worship*)

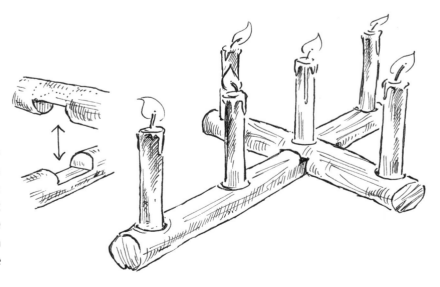

Grace before a meal

For these and all your gifts
We thank you Lord. Amen.

Thoughts for food

Vegetable hot pot

You will need:
- 3 large onions
- 1 small green pepper
- 1 good sized aubergine
- 4 tbsp cooking oil
- 450 g (1 lb) ripe tomatoes or a 400 g (14 oz) tin of tomatoes

- 1 clove of garlic
- 1 tsp sugar
- 1 bay leaf
- ½ tsp basil
- salt and black pepper

1. Peel the onions and cut them into chunks. Cut the green pepper into very small pieces and the aubergine into 1 or 2 cm cubes. Skin and roughly chop the tomatoes. Crush the garlic.
2. Heat the oil in a large heavy-based pan and turn the onions over in it for a couple of minutes.
3. Add the pepper and the aubergine and mix well, then add the tomatoes, garlic, sugar, salt, bay leaf, basil and a good grating of black pepper and mix it all together well.
4. Cover tightly and simmer very gently for at least half an hour; an hour is not too long to cook this dish. Serve with rice or pasta or large chunks of crusty bread.

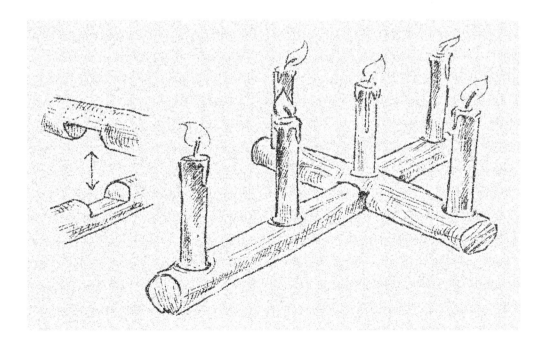

Lent
The following weeks

Colour: purple

Background

Lent is a season of 40 days that looks forward and prepares for a future celebration – the Easter vigil and the whole of the Easter season. Lent is a time when we can reflect upon the things that prevent us turning to God. As we enter the wilderness with Christ, the Church invites us to travel light, and to live lives of simplicity. Our homes should reflect this theme, giving space for quiet and stillness. Lent can be embraced as a time for making space in busy lives to focus on welcoming the risen Christ once again into our lives and homes. The following chapter includes some of the ideas which we have used during Lent.

Bible readings

The First Sunday of Lent

Year A	Year B	Year C
Genesis 2.15-17; 3.1-7	Genesis 9.8-17	Deuteronomy 26.1-11
Romans 5.12-19	1 Peter 3.18-22	Romans 10.8b-13
Matthew 4.1-11	Mark 1.9-15	Luke 4.1-13

The Second Sunday of Lent

Year A	Year B	Year C
Genesis 12.1-14a	Genesis 17.1-7,15-16	Genesis 15.1-12,17-18
Romans 4.1-5,13-17	Romans 4.13-25	Philippians 13.17-19.1
John 3.1-17	Mark 8.31-38	Luke 13.31-35

The Third Sunday of Lent

Year A	Year B	Year C
Exodus 17.1-7	Exodus 20.1-17	Isaiah 55.1-9
Romans 5.1-11	1 Corinthians 1.18-25	1 Corinthians 10.1-13
John 4.5-42	John 2.13-22	Luke 13.1-9

The Fourth Sunday of Lent

Year A	Year B	Year C
1 Samuel 16.1-13	Numbers 21.4-9	Joshua 5.9-12
Ephesians 5.8-14	Ephesians 2.1-10	2 Corinthians 5.16-21
John 9.1-41	John 13.14-21	Luke 15.1-3,11b-32

The Fifth Sunday of Lent

Year A	Year B	Year C
Ezekiel 37.1-14	Jeremiah 31.31-34	Isaiah 43.16-21
Romans 8.6-11	Hebrews 5.5-10	Philippians 3.4b-14
John 11.1-45	John 12.20-33	John 12.1-8

Prayer

The First Sunday of Lent

Almighty God,
whose Son Jesus Christ fasted forty days in the
    wilderness,
and was tempted as we are, yet without sin:
give us grace to discipline ourselves
    in obedience to your Spirit;
and, as you know our weakness,
so may we know your power to save;
through Jesus Christ your Son our Lord,
who is alive and reigns with you,
in the unity of the Holy Spirit,
one God, now and for ever. Amen.

The Second Sunday of Lent

Almighty God,
you show to those who are in error the light
    of your truth,
that they may return to the way of
    righteousness:
grant to all those who are admitted
    into the fellowship of Christ's religion,
that they may reject those things
    that are contrary to their profession,
and follow all such things as are agreeable
    to the same;
through our Lord Jesus Christ,
who is alive and reigns with you,
in the unity of the Holy Spirit,
one God, now and for ever. Amen.

The Third Sunday of Lent

Almighty God,
whose most dear Son went not up to joy
    but first he suffered pain,
and entered not into glory before he was
    crucified;
mercifully grant that we, walking in the way
    of the cross,
may find it none other than the way of life
    and peace;
through Jesus Christ your Son our Lord,
who is alive and reigns with you,
in the unity of the Holy Spirit,
one God, now and for ever. Amen.

The Fourth Sunday of Lent

Merciful Lord,
absolve your people from their offences,
that through your bountiful goodness
we may all be delivered from the chains of
    those sins
which by our frailty we have committed;
grant this, heavenly Father,
for Jesus Christ's safe, our blessed Lord and
    Saviour,
who is alive and reigns with you,
in the unity of the Holy Spirit,
one God, now and for ever. Amen.

The Fifth Sunday of Lent

Most merciful God,
who by the death and resurrection
    of your Son Jesus Christ
delivered and saved the world:
grant that by faith in him who suffered on the
    cross
we may triumph in the power of his victory;
through Jesus Christ your Son our Lord,
who is alive and reigns with you,
in the unity of the Holy Spirit,
one God, now and for ever. Amen.

(all from *Common Worship*)

Grace before a meal

This is sung to the tune of 'Amazing Grace'.

O, thank you Lord
for all our food;
you call,
you guide,
you feed.
Help us to share
your love and care
with those who are in need. Amen.

(from *Reign Dance*)

Activity

Redemption calendar

A redemption calendar can be used in the last two weeks before Easter Day, from Passion Sunday onwards. The calendar takes the shape of an ark – one of the symbols of the Church. One window can be opened during each day's prayer time, and the passage from scripture seen in the window can be read.

You will need two large A1 sheets of card and materials for decorating.

Draw a large ark on one sheet of card, adding 14 windows, and one large door that is used for Easter Day. Place the second sheet of card under the first one and mark out the position of the windows and door with a pencil. Draw, in each of these boxes, one Bible reference along with the appropriate picture.

References for making a redemption calendar
The calendar starts two weeks before Easter Day.

Sunday	The wedding at Cana	John 2.1-11
Monday	Throwing the traders out of the Temple	John 2.13-22
Tuesday	Living water from the well	John 4.5-42
Wednesday	Healing the cripple by the pool	John 5.2-21
Thursday	Feeding of the 5000	John 6.1-15
Friday	Healing of the blind man	John 9.1-7
Saturday	The raising of Lazarus	John 11.1-45
Palm Sunday	Entry into Jerusalem	Mark 11.1-10
Monday	Betrayal by Judas	Matthew 26.1-5,14-16,20-25
Tuesday	Agony in the Garden	Mark 14.12-16,22-25
Wednesday	Washing of the feet	John 13.1-16
Maundy Thursday	The Last Supper	Mark 14.32-42
Good Friday	Crucifixion	Luke 23.33-46
Holy Saturday	Sealed tomb	Luke 23.50-56
Easter Sunday	Empty tomb	Matthew 28.1-10

Preparing the home

The Lenten Tree

Lent, like Advent, is a time of preparation and waiting. As with the Jesse Tree in Advent, so a Lenten Tree can visibly show the promises God has made to us.

Given below are Bible references and appropriate symbols to represent God's promises. The symbols could be made using sheets of card and felt-tip pens and crayons to draw and colour the symbols.

In our family we read the Bible reference and then hang the symbol on a branch, and finish off with a prayer. An alternative would be to draw the outline of a tree on a large piece of paper or card (strips of plain wallpaper would do) and stick the symbols on the tree using Blu-Tack.

Promises	Symbol	Reference
Of salvation	The cross	Colossians 1.19,20
	Lamb	John 1.29
	Fish (icthus)	Jesus Christ, Son of God, Saviour
	Rainbow	Genesis 9.13
	Washing powder	Isaiah 1.18
To give light	Candle	John 8.12
	Sun	Genesis 1.3
	Moon	Genesis 1.5
To guide	Feet	Psalm 18.33
	Door	John 10.7
	Signpost	John 14.6
To save	Shepherd's crook	Psalm 23.1/John 10.14
	Arms	Deuteronomy 33.27
	Hen and chicks	Luke 13.34
	A heart (symbol of friendship)	John 15.14
	Doctor's bag (symbol of healing)	Jeremiah 33.6
	River	Jeremiah 31.9b
	Mountains	Psalm 121.1,2
	Holy Spirit (H.S.)	John 14.26
To provide for physical needs	Bread	John 6.35
	Wine	Matthew 26.27,28
	Water	John 4.14
	Bird (sparrow)	Matthew 10.29
	Lily	Luke 12.27
To teach	Blackboard	Psalm 119.171
	Ear	Isaiah 30.21
	Vine	John 15.1
	Bible	Psalm 119.89
Of peace	Olive branch	Genesis 8.11
	Dove	John 1.32
Of the kingdom	Trumpets	1 Corinthians 15.52
	Someone singing	Isaiah 12.5
	Praying hands	Matthew 6.6
	Church	Matthew 6.18
	Treasure	Matthew 13.45,46
	Fishing nets	Matthew 13.47,48
Pictures of God	Crown/king	Malachi 1.14b
	Rock	Psalm 18.2
	Alpha/beginning	Revelation 21.6
	Omega/end	Revelation 22.13
	Manger/Emmanuel	Matthew 1.23
	Fire	Hebrews 12.29
	Father	Matthew 6.9
	Ring/bridegroom	Revelation 18.23
	Scales/justice	Ezekiel 20.36
	Towel/servant	Luke 22.7

Thoughts for food

Passiontide biscuits

These biscuits can be made and hung on a branch every day for the last two weeks of Lent. This two-week period is known as Passiontide, when we turn our thoughts to the last days of Jesus' earthly life.

You will need:

> 175 g (6 oz) wholemeal flour
> 75 g (3 oz) butter
> 50 g (2 oz) ground almonds
> 2 tbsp caster sugar
> 1 egg, separated
> cold water
> 225 g (8 oz) icing sugar
> tubes of coloured icing
> assorted colours of fine ribbon

1. Pre heat oven to 175°C (350°F, gas mark 4) and grease several baking sheets.
2. Sieve the flour into a bowl and rub in the butter until the mixture resembles breadcrumbs. Stir in the ground almonds, sugar, the egg yolk and enough cold water to form a soft dough.
3. Knead the dough and roll it out thinly, then cut into 14 rounds using a biscuit cutter. Arrange the biscuits on the prepared baking sheets and make a hole in the top of each one using a drinking straw.
4. Bake for 10–15 minutes or until lightly browned. Cool on a wire rack.
5. When cold, mix the egg white and icing sugar together to make an icing to cover the biscuits.
6. Dip the surface of each biscuit into the mixture and leave to dry.
7. When the icing is dry and hard use the tubes of icing to ice numbers 1–14 on them. Thread ribbons through the holes at the top and hand a biscuit out each day until Easter Day. (Adapted from *The Complete Interactive Cookbook*, 1996, Softkey Multimedia, under the title 'Advent Cookies'.)

In our family we use green icing for numbers 1–11; Good Friday (number 12) is in black icing, number 13 (Holy Saturday) is in red and Easter Day (number 14) is piped in yellow icing with a design to correspond to Easter. One year we piped crosses, another year a rising sun.

Food for thought

✦ Remember times when you found it easy and difficult to pray. What were the times and what happened?

✦ Think about a time when someone was loving and forgiving to you. God is loving and forgiving. Is there anything he can't forgive and why?

✦ What makes you angry?

✦ When do you get angry with God? Are there situations and things in the world that make you angry?

Annunciation

of our Lord to the Blessed Virgin Mary

Colour: gold or white

Background

On 25th March we celebrate the Annunciation of Jesus to Mary. It is a day when we give thanks for Mary's decision to say 'yes' to God and to accept what he wanted her to do. Nine months from this date the Church will celebrate the birth of Jesus. In this chapter are a couple of ideas that we have used as a family to celebrate the Annunciation.

Bible readings

Isaiah 7.10-14
Hebrews 10.4-10
Luke 1.26-38

Prayer

We beseech you, O Lord,
pour your grace into our hearts,
that as we have known the incarnation
  of your Son Jesus Christ
by the message of an angel,
so by his cross and passion
we may be brought to the glory of his
  resurrection;
through Jesus Christ your Son our Lord,
who is alive and reigns with you,
in the unity of the Holy Spirit,
one God, now and forever. Amen.

(Collect for the Annunciation of Our Lord
from *Common Worship*)

Grace before a meal

For the food before us
and the person beside us
we give you thanks, O Lord. Amen.

Activity

Annunciation greetings card puzzle

You will need:

an old Christmas card with a picture of the Annunciation or of angels.
a piece of card to stick your picture on
glue
scissors
felt-tip pens
pencils
ruler.

Take your picture and stick it onto your piece of card. Using your pencil very lightly draw the shapes you want to make your puzzle card into. You might want to cut it into squares or crazy shapes. Before you cut it into shapes, write a greeting on the back. Then cut it into pieces, carefully following the pencil lines. When you've done that put your puzzle into an envelope and send your greetings to a friend.

Thoughts for food

Angel cake

40 g (1½ oz) plain flour
100 g (4 oz) caster sugar
4 egg whites
pinch of salt
½ tsp cream of tartar
2 drops vanilla essence
300 ml (½ pint) whipping cream, whipped
225 g (8 oz) frozen raspberries, thawed and drained
1 litre (1¾ pint) deep, fluted ring mould or angel cake tin, greased
a piping bag with a star nozzle

1. Set the oven at 190°C (375°F, gas mark 5).
2. Sieve the flour with half of the caster sugar three times and set aside.
3. Whisk the egg whites with the salt and cream of tartar until they form soft peaks.
4. Whisk in the vanilla essence and remaining sugar in batches, two tablespoons at a time, until the mixture stands in firm peaks.
5. Fold in the flour and sugar mixture.
6. Spoon into the tin and bake for 30–35 minutes until springy to the touch.
7. Turn the cake, still in the tin, upside down on a wire rack and leave to cool completely before lifting off the tin.
8. Cut the cake in half horizontally and fill and decorate with whipped cream and thawed raspberries. Serve at once.

Food for thought

✦ Think about the times when people have been messengers, angels, who have given you God's good news?

✦ If you were to draw a picture of God what would it be like?

✦ What are the ways in which we say 'yes' to the call of God? What about us needs to change, at home, school, work or community, for us to be able to do this?

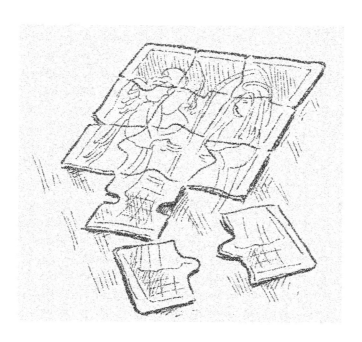

Palm Sunday

Colour: red

Background

Palm Sunday is the day that begins Holy Week. On this day the Church recalls Jesus' entry in Jerusalem on a donkey, when the crowds waved palm branches and placed them in his path crying 'Hosanna to the Son of David' (Matthew 21.1-15).

In many churches this event is re-enacted by the giving of palms and by taking part in a procession in the streets around the church. This reminds us that we follow a God who overcame suffering and death to reign triumphant. This day sets the stage for the dramatic events of Holy Week and invites us to partake in the drama.

At home we like to create something of a festive air with a banner and a palm archway. You will find these ideas in *Preparing the home* and *Activities*.

Bible readings

The readings for today reflect the two events in Jesus' life: that of riding into Jerusalem on a donkey and being hailed by the crowd with palm branches, and also looking to his trial and death.

Prayer

Almighty and everlasting God,
who in your tender love towards the human race
   sent your Son our Saviour Jesus Christ
to take upon him our flesh
and to suffer death upon the cross:
grant that we may follow the example of his
   patience and humility,
and also be made partakers of his resurrection;
through Jesus Christ your Son our Lord,
who is alive and reigns with you,
in the unity of the Holy Spirit,
one God, now and for ever. Amen.

(Collect for Palm Sunday from *Common Worship*)

Grace before a meal

This is sung to the tune of 'The Archers'.

Roast potatoes; sticks and worms,
Cabbage from the garden;
Gravy, stuffing, veggie bake;
Fruit or chocolate cake . . .
Lord, you water us,
Love and talk to us,
Tend and nurture with pride.
So, in awe, we thank you for
God to fill us inside!

(from *Reign Dance*)

Year A	Year B	Year C
Liturgy of the palms	**Liturgy of the palms**	**Liturgy of the palms**
Matthew 21.1-11	Mark 11.1-11	Luke 19.28-40
Liturgy of the Passion	**Liturgy of the Passion**	**Liturgy of the Passion**
Isaiah 50.4-9a	Isaiah 50.4-9a	Isaiah 50.4-9a
Philippians 2.5-11	Philippians 2.5-11	Philippians 2.5-11
Matthew 27.11-54	Mark 15.1-39	Luke 23.1-49

Preparing the home
Palm branch door arch

Making a palm arch for your front door will be a reminder of Jesus' entry through the gate into Jerusalem. It also reminds us that as we enter out homes we should make them places of truth and integrity, where we can worship God, who we hail as king. For the palm arch you will need:

> large sheets of card or stiff paper
> scissors
> Blu-Tack
> paints and crayons, etc. (optional).

Cut out two palm branch shapes, as in the template above, big enough to reach from the bottom to the top of your front door. Score down the centre of each branch and fold back gently until the palm has a slight curve. Decoration can be added to the branch to make it a bit more special. When the branch is complete, stick it to the door frame with Blu-Tack.

Alternatively, the door can be decorated using greenery from the garden. You might also like to place the palm crosses that you received at church in a prominent place in your home.

Activity
Palm Sunday banner

You will need:
> a large piece of paper (e.g. two pieces of wall-paper stuck together with sellotape – plain side out)
> coloured paper or felt
> scissors
> glue
> felt-tip pens.

Write and cut out the letters to make the words 'Hosanna to the king of kings!' Cut them out, arrange and stick them onto the banner. Then cut out a crown shape and palm branches.

Place the crown and branches on the banner and stick in place.

In our family we usually hang our banner in the dining room and sing a verse from our favourite Palm Sunday hymn as part of our meal-time grace.

Thoughts for food

Cheese and courgette tart

4 large tomatoes, sliced
2 courgettes, thinly sliced
1 tsp dried marjoram and thyme
40 g (1½ oz) margarine or butter
175 g (6 oz) plain flour
40 g (1½ oz) cheddar cheese, grated
a pinch of mustard powder
a pinch of salt and pepper

1. Pre-heat the oven to 200°C (400°F, gas mark 6). Grease and line a 25 cm (10 in) shallow sponge tin. Arrange the tomatoes on the edge of the tin with the courgettes in the middle and marjoram and thyme sprinkled over.
2. Rub the butter or margarine into the flour. Add the cheese, mustard powder and seasoning and 1 tsp cold water. Form the dough into a ball and knead lightly.
3. Roll the pastry to the size of the tin then lift and place it on top of the tomatoes and courgettes. Bake for 40 minutes, then cool for 5 minutes before turning out and removing the paper lining. Serve with a salad.

Food for thought

✦ Remember a time when you told the truth but were not believed. What happened and what did it feel like?

✦ When I hear that Jesus is king it makes me think of ...

✦ Re-read the story of the entry of Jesus into Jerusalem. What do you like about the story and why? If you could have been there, where would you have been standing and why?

Maundy Thursday

Colour: White or Gold

Background

Maundy Thursday eve marks the beginning of the Easter Triduum – the three great days of Good Friday, Holy Saturday and Easter Day. These three days form a continuum and are the culmination of the Church's year. The day takes its name from the Latin word 'mandatum', meaning commandment, and refers to the words that Jesus gave to his disciples after he washed their feet at the Last Supper: 'a new commandment I give to you, that you love one another, as I have loved you', John 13.34. Jesus shows us his sacrificial love and invites us into this way of loving.

Maundy Thursday also holds within it the theme of the institution of the Lord's Supper. On this day we remember the events surrounding the disciples and Jesus at a Passover meal on the night he was betrayed, where Jesus spoke words contained in every eucharistic prayer: 'This is my body ... this is my blood ... do this in remembrance of me'.

It is for this reason that we have included a form for a Christian Passover meal. The Jewish beginning of the day is in the evening and so Maundy Thursday is linked into what happens on Good Friday.

Worship runs in unbroken form from this day to Easter Day, following the events in the last days of Jesus' life.

At home we spend the day getting ready to participate in a Christian Passover meal, an example of which can be found in this chapter.

Bible readings

Exodus 12.1-8,11-14
1 Corinthians 11.23-29
John 13.1-15

Prayer

God our Father
you have invited us to share
   in the supper
which your Son gave to his Church
to proclaim his death until he comes:
may he nourish us by his presence,
and unite us in his love;
who is alive and reigns with you,
in the unity of the Holy Spirit,
one God, now and for ever. Amen.

(Collect for Maundy Thursday from *Common Worship*)

Grace before a meal

Blessed are you Lord God of all creation
Through your goodness we have this food,
Which earth has given and human hands have made.
Blessed be God forever. Amen.

(adapted from *Common Worship*)

Preparing the home

Maundy Thursday could be used as a time for 'spring-cleaning'. Anything that underlines our spiritual life and points towards the new life of Easter is the theme here. Washing the curtains, polishing the furniture or cleaning the windows helps us to get ourselves ready for the feast of Easter.

For the Christian Passover meal you may wish to decorate the table. You could include: candles on the table to signify Christ as the light of the world; a dish of grapes to signify wine; a bowl of olives to signify the oil of healing; and a dried flower arrangement, which could include wheat to signify the bread, and bulrushes as a symbol of the Old Testament figure of Moses.

Activities
Kim's Passover game
You will need:

a tray
a cloth
items to represent the Passion, e.g. silver coins
– to represent 30 pieces of silver
3 nails
a hammer
pliers
purple cloth
dice
a thorny branch
a sponge
vinegar
knotted string – to represent the 'whip'
a wooden cross
a toy cockerel
a jar of ointment
a small bowl of water, etc.

Put all the items on the tray and cover with the cloth. Each player in turn has 10 seconds to look at the items. The cloth is then replaced, and the player recalls as many items on the tray as possible.

This game can be extended by asking what each item represents and where it comes in the Passion story.

Silver coins = 30 pieces of silver; 3 nails = the nails that were knocked into the cross; hammer = to knock in the nails; pliers = to take the nails out of the cross; purple cloth = Jesus was mocked as king of the Jews, the purple cloth was worn by high-ranking officials or royalty; dice = Jesus' clothing was gambled for by the Roman soldiers, they rolled dice to see who would keep his robe; thorny branch = to represent the crown of thorns; sponge, vinegar = whilst on the cross, Jesus was offered a drink of sour wine or vinegar, which was soaked on a sponge; knotted string = to represent the whip with which Jesus was tortured before

execution; wooden cross = the cross; toy cockerel = Peter denied Jesus three times before the cock crowed; jar of ointment = Jesus' body was anointed with ointment after death; bowl of water = Pilate washed his hands at the trial of Jesus.

Hide and seek

Before the meal begins, an adult hides one piece of unleavened bread. At the end of the meal the children search for it. The game reminds us that we seek for God as God seeks for us.

Thoughts for food
Christian Passover meal
You will need for the Christian Passover meal:

candles
red wine
a bowl of warm water and a towel
unleavened bread, e.g. matzos
parsley and a small bowl of salt water
lamb or vegetarian equivalent
vegetables and salad, etc.
charoseth (pronounced 'haroset').

The unleavened bread represents the bread made in a hurry when the Jews left for Egypt; the wine and roast lamb represent the lamb that was killed and its blood sprinkled on the doorposts, so that God would know which houses to pass over and leave alone; the parsley stands for the bitter herbs, to signify the bitterness of life in enslavement. The parsley is dipped in salt water to represent tears; the charoseth is like the cement that held together the bricks the Israelites made in captivity.

Here is a recipe for charoseth for four to five people:

    225 g (8 oz) eating apples
    175 g (6 oz) nuts, chopped
    4 tbsp honey
    2 tbsp sugar
    125 ml (4 fl oz) sweet red wine
    3-4 tsp cinnamon

1. Peel and grate the apples.
2. Mix the apples and nuts and add the cinnamon.
3. Stir in the honey and sugar and enough wine to make a stiff paste.

Grace

Glasses are filled with wine and raised:

> Blessed are you, Lord, God of all creation.
> Through your goodness we have this wine, fruit of the vine and work of human hands.
> Blessed are you for choosing us to be your holy people.
> Blessed are you for letting us live to celebrate this feast.
> Blessed be God for ever.
> **Blessed be God for ever. Amen.**

(from H. J. Richards, *The Passover Meal*)

Leaders all drink and refill their glasses

Starters

Part of the tradition of Maundy Thursday is the washing of feet. In place of this at the meal table, you may wish to wash one another's hands. For this you will need a large bowl, warm water and a towel, and optional scented oil for the water.

After this, take the parsley and dip it in the salt water. Take the bread, keeping a small portion aside for the unexpected guest.

An adult: Blessed are you, Lord, God of all creation.
             Through your goodness we have this bread,
             which earth has given and human hands have made.
             Let all who are hungry come and share this food with us.

The story

A young person asks the questions:

> Why is this night different from all other nights?
>
> What did Jesus tell his friends to do?

Here we tell the story of our ancestors' journey from slavery through the wilderness and into the promised land. We give witness to our connection to this journey of the Hebrews. We can do this by using language that is personal and real to those present, for example:

We were slaves in Egypt; oppressed by Pharoah. Our God brought us safely out of Egypt. This fulfilled the promises that our God made to our father Abraham when he was asked to journey into the wilderness.

It was on the night of the Passover that Jesus broke bread and poured wine with his disciples for our salvation. He washed his disciples' feet as a servant would have done, and showed us God's generous love.

You may wish to use biblical material to re-tell the story, for example Deuteronomy 26.5-9 or Isaiah 43.1-4. At the end of the story the blessing is said over the wine in thankfulness for being delivered from oppression to freedom.

Leader: Blessed are you, Lord, God of all creation,
           who created the fruit of the vine to rejoice our hearts.
           Blessed be God for ever.

All: **Blessed be God for ever.**

All drink a second glass of wine.

The meal

We eat the symbolic food laid out on the table: the bitter herbs eaten with matzos, a sign of the bitterness of slavery; and the charoseth, a sign of the sweetness of freedom and the goodness of God. The main meal is then served. This is traditionally a leg of lamb. For those who are vegetarian an alternative can be substituted.

At the end of the meal the remaining portion of bread is taken and eaten by everyone. An extra glass is filled for the prophet Elijah. Elijah is seen both in the Old Testament and in the New as the herald of the kingdom. He is the forerunner of the Messiah, and we welcome him as a guest.

One of the children goes to the front door to inform the family whether he has arrived.

Grace after the meal

All glasses are then filled, and the following grace is said:

> We give thanks to God for he is good.
> All creatures look to you, Lord, and you
> give them their food in due season,
> you open your hand and they have their fill.
> Blessed be God for ever. Amen.

All drink the third cup of wine.

The meal ends with all joining hands and saying:

> The Grace of our Lord Jesus Christ, and the love of God, and the fellowship of the Holy Spirit, be with us all, evermore. Amen.

(adapted from H. J. Richards, *The Passover Meal*)

Food for thought

✦ Remember times and people who have shown you the love of God. In what ways can we pass God's love on to other people?

✦ Have you ever been betrayed by a friend and have you ever betrayed a friend? What did it feel like?

✦ Think about where you live and the church you attend. What places help you to pray? Do you like to pray outside? What change could you make to your home that would help you in prayer?

Good Friday

Colour: red

Background

On Good Friday afternoon we mark the event of the death of Jesus on the cross. Traditionally, the events leading to the crucifixion have been read from St John's Gospel, which stresses the victory of the cross. It is a day that the Church sets aside for us to reflect upon the meaning of the cross in our own lives and be challenged by it, aided by silence and reflection. This day is referred to as 'Good' because the sacrificial love of Jesus on the cross made possible the salvation of all people.

The Church makes provision for a service of Veneration of the Cross with its emphasis on what God has done for us, that he reigns as Lord and king. In our family we eat hot cross buns at breakfast on Good Friday. After attending church we may go for a walk, using this as an opportunity to look for sticks and twigs to make into crosses.

Bible readings

Isaiah 52.13
Hebrews 10.16-25
John 18,19

Prayer

Almighty Father,
look with mercy on this your family
for which our Lord Jesus Christ
    was content to be betrayed
    and given up into the hands of sinners
    and to suffer death upon the cross;
who is alive and glorified with you and
    the Holy Spirit,
one God, now and for ever. Amen.

(Collect for Good Friday
from *Common Worship*)

Grace before a meal

Be present at our table, Lord,
Be here and everywhere adored
Thy creatures bless and grant that we
May feast in paradise with thee. Amen.

(John Wesley, 1703–92)

Activity
A Good Friday cross

You will need several large cardboard boxes (all the same size, e.g. wine boxes or shoe boxes), at least four for the vertical and two for the cross pieces, which can be sellotaped together to make a cross shape.

The whole of the cross is then covered in plain paper, or painted white. Have plenty of newspapers and magazines that you can look at and choose pictures and headlines which best illustrate themes for Good Friday, such as death, loss and darkness. We see these through war, destruction, poverty, desolation, suffering, illness and homelessness.

Encourage your children to talk about these events with you as you cut out the pictures and try to relate them to Jesus' death on the cross. Stick the pictures and words onto the cross, adding anything else you feel is fitting using felt-tip pens. Stand the cross in a prominent place, e.g. the hallway, for all to look at as they spend the rest of the day in and around the home.

Thoughts for food

Hot cross buns

These are good to eat for breakfast on Good Friday.

You will need:

150 g (6 oz) strong white flour
150 g (6 oz) strong wholemeal flour
1 tsp salt
1 tbsp mixed spice
50 g (2 oz) soft light brown sugar
50 g (2 oz) butter
150 g (5 oz) currants
50 g (2 oz) mixed candied peel
1 sachet easy blend yeast
300 ml (½ pint) milk
2 medium eggs, beaten.

For the crosses:
125 g (4½ oz) plain white flour
45 ml (2 fl oz) vegetable oil

For the glaze:
2 tbsp clear honey, warmed

This mixture makes approximately 22 buns.

1. Preheat the oven to 200°C (400°F, gas mark 6).
2. Place the flours, salt, spice and sugar in a bowl. Rub in the butter, and add the currants and peel. Then stir in the yeast.
3. Warm the milk until you are still just able to put your finger into it, then add it to the flour mixture with the eggs. Mix well to form a dough.
4. Turn onto a floured surface and knead lightly until smooth and elastic, about 10 minutes.
5. Place the dough in a clean bowl, cover and leave to rise in a warm place for an hour, until doubled in size.
6. Turn out onto a floured surface and knead again for 2 minutes.
7. Divide the dough into 22 pieces and form into balls. Place on an oiled baking sheet and mark a cross on top of each bun with a sharp knife. Cover and leave in a warm place for 20–30 minutes until doubled in size again.
8. Mix together the flour, oil and 90 ml (3 fl oz) cold water. Using a piping bag, pipe a cross onto the buns.
9. Cook for 15 minutes, or until brown.
10. When cooked, brush the buns with warm honey and allow to cool on a wire rack.

Food for thought

✦ Think of a place or situation where God's love is needed. What needs to happen?

✦ How can we make a difference?

✦ Think of times when God might feel sad, disappointed and hurt?

✦ Remember a time when you were lonely and alone. When was it and what did it feel like? What happened next?

Holy Saturday

Background

On this day the Church waits by the tomb where Jesus has been laid, reflecting on his suffering and death.

There is the tradition of a Vigil Service late on this day. This service has four different elements.

1. The Service of Light, where from a blessed new fire the Easter (paschal) candle is lit and borne in procession into a dark church that proclaims the Resurrection – Christ our light risen from the darkness of the tomb. At the end of this procession the ancient Exultet (Easter song) is sung.
2. The vigil, where our faith journey is revealed through readings from the Old Testament and New Testament.
3. The baptism, where we renew our baptismal vows, and where baptisms in the early Church traditionally took place.
4. The Eucharist, where we celebrate the first communion of Easter and we are sacramentally united with the risen Christ.

On Holy Saturday we begin to get our home ready for Easter Day. During Lent and especially Holy Week the feeling is quieter and more reflective, but on Holy Saturday we begin by bringing the first spring flowers into our home, by decorating eggs for an Easter branch and creating an Easter garden.

Bible readings
Exultet

The Exultet can be used in the home as one would use a scriptural reading. It may be read as a piece of poetry on one's own or together with others. It may also be used as the basis for prayer time by taking one or two sentences and expanding them into prayers of praise and thanksgiving. Parts of the Exultet may inspire artwork that can be used creatively in the home.

Rejoice, heavenly powers!
Sing, choirs of angels!
Exult, all creation around God's throne!
Jesus Christ, our King, is risen!
Sound the trumpet of salvation!

Rejoice, O earth, in shining splendour,
radiant in the brightness of your King!
Christ has conquered! Glory fills you!
Darkness vanishes for ever!

Rejoice, O Mother Church! Exult in glory!
The risen Saviour shines upon you!
Let this place resound with joy,
echoing the mighty song of all God's people!

It is indeed right
that with full hearts and minds and voices
we should praise you, the unseen God,
    the Father Almighty,
and your only Son, Jesus Christ our Lord,
who has ransomed us by his death,
and paid for us the price of Adam's sin.

For this is the Passover of that true Lamb of God,
by whose blood the homes of all the faithful
are hallowed and protected.

This is the night when of old you saved
    our fathers,
delivering the people of Israel from their slavery,
and leading them dry-shod through the sea.

This is the night when Jesus Christ
    vanquished hell
and rose triumphant from the grave.

This is the night when all who believe in him are
    freed from sin
and restored to grace and holiness.

Most blessed of all nights,
when wickedness is put to flight
    and sin is washed away,
lost innocence regained,
    and mourning turned to joy.

Night truly blessed,
when heaven is wedded to earth
and all creation reconciled to God!

Therefore heavenly Father, in the joy of
this night,
accept our sacrifice of praise,
your Church's solemn offering;
and grant that this Easter candle
may make our darkness light;
for Christ the Morning Star has risen,
never again to set,
and is alive and reigns for ever and ever. Amen.

(Lent, Holy Week, Easter, p. 230)

At the vigil some of the following readings are used:

Genesis 1.1-2.4a
Genesis 7.1-5,11-18; 8.6-18; 9.8-13
Genesis 22.1-18
Exodus 14.10-31; 15.20-21
Isaiah 55.1-11
Proverbs 8.1-8, 19-21; 9.4b-6
Ezekiel 36.24-28
Ezekiel 37.1-14
Zephaniah 3.14-20
Romans 6.3-11

Year A	Year B	Year C
Matthew 28.1-10	Mark 16.1-8	Luke 24.1-12

Prayer

Grant, Lord,
that we who are baptized into the death
of your Son our Saviour Jesus Christ
may continually put to death our evil desires
and be buried with him;
and that through the grave and gate of death
we may pass to our joyful resurrection;
through his merits, who died and was buried
and rose again for us,
your Son Jesus Christ our Lord. Amen.

(Collect for Easter Eve from Common Worship)

Grace before a meal

For the food before us
and the person beside us
we give you thanks, O Lord. Amen.

Preparing the home
Easter garland

This is a good day to make a garland in preparation for Easter. You will need some rope (a piece of washing line is a good thickness) and crepe or tissue paper in green and various other colours.

First you need to cut the green paper into strips, which you wind around the rope to completely cover it. Hold the paper in place using sellotape. Then cut out green leaf shapes and circles of other colours.

Put two or three circles of coloured paper together, mixing the colours, e.g. pink, purple and yellow, and by twisting the centres together you can create a flower shape. Attach the leaves and flowers onto the covered rope with sellotape at intervals all along the rope to create a garland.

On Easter morning you may like to hang this around the cross you made on Good Friday to show that the cross of suffering and shame has become the 'Tree of Life'.

Easter branch

Holy Saturday is also a good time to begin to decorate our homes to celebrate Easter. We can do this by choosing two or three branches that have blossom or newly opened leaves and placing then in a vase. These can be hung with decorated eggs, fluffy chicks and bows.

To decorate eggs, they first need to be blown by making a small hole at the top and bottom and blowing the yolk etc. through one of the holes. The eggs are then rinsed and cleaned. When they are dry they can be decorated in numerous ways. You can stick on pictures from old cards, or transfers can be bought from craft shops. You can dye them in different colours or simply paint them using poster paints. Whatever you choose to use they will look festive for Easter Day.

Easter table cloth

You will need either white paper or a cloth, large enough to cover your table. Decorate with symbols of Easter using fabric paints, felt-tip pens, cloth or paper shapes. Use the tablecloth as part of the Easter Day celebrations.

Alternatively you can make a doodle tablecloth on Easter Day. You will need a large sheet of paper for the tablecloth and wax crayons or felt-tip pens. Decorate, write and doodle on the tablecloth before and during the meal using words and images of the Easter season.

The decorated cloths may be used to begin discussion about what the season means to you personally. It could even be used afterwards to decorate the wall. Whatever you decide, have fun!

Activities

Easter garden and dolly peg people

You may like to make an Easter garden. If you have a small corner free in your garden you can plant some small conifers for trees and create a tomb using stones. You can add other plants such as primulas. People can be added using dolly pegs dressed in scraps of material, with paper wings added for the angel at the tomb.

Take some twigs and bind them together to make three crosses and set these up in the background. Encourage the children to dig and plant and to place the plants and stones. They can also have fun creating the 'dolly peg' disciples and angel. This should create opportunities for discussion about what happened on the first Easter Day and very young children may want to act it out with the 'dolly peg' people. If you don't have a garden you can do this in a deep roasting tin or a cardboard box lined with a bin liner. If you do this indoors you may like to place it near the cross made on Good Friday.

Decorating a paschal candle

A candle which you can light on Easter Day and at mealtimes during the Easter season can provide a focus in the days after Easter Day. You need a large fat round candle big enough to paint or stick on a paper design. Poster paint, used thickly, will stick to the wax surface.

The Greek symbols Α for alpha and Ω for omega, which are the first and last letters of the Greek alphabet, can be used to represent Jesus Christ who said 'I am the Alpha and the Omega, the beginning and the end'. The date can also be added.

Thoughts for food

Simnel cake

This is traditionally eaten on Mothering Sunday, but can also be prepared on Holy Saturday to eat on Easter Day. You will need:

225 g (8 oz) butter or margarine
225 g (8 oz) light soft brown sugar
5 medium eggs, beaten
350 g (12 oz) plain white flour
1 tsp nutmeg
1 tsp cinnamon
275 g (10 oz) sultanas
275 g (10 oz) raisins
275 g (10 oz) glacé cherries, halved
175 g (6 oz) dried apricots, chopped
250 g (9 oz) white marzipan

For the decoration:
1 tbsp apricot jam
725 g (1½ lb) white marzipan
1 medium egg, beaten

1. Preheat the oven to 150°C (300°F, gas mark 2). Grease and line a 20 cm (8 in) deep round cake tin.
2. Cream the butter or margarine and sugar in a bowl until light and fluffy.
3. Beat in the eggs and flour, then add the nutmeg and cinnamon.
4. Stir in the sultanas, raisins, cherries and apricots.
5. Cut the marzipan into 1 cm chunks and stir them into the mixture. Spoon into the prepared tin and level out.
6. Cover the cake with greaseproof paper. Bake for 3 hours, then remove the paper and cook for a further hour. Remove the cake from the oven and cool slightly, then turn out the cake to cool completely.
7. When cold, warm the jam and brush it over the top of the cake.
8. Next, divide the marzipan into three. Roll out one piece and cut out a 17.5 cm circle; gently lift it on to the cake.
9. From the second piece roll out two long thin lengths. Twist these together and place around the top of the cake, pressing to seal.
10. Divide the remaining marzipan into 11 balls. Place around the top of the cake, sticking them in place with a little jam. Brush the top with a little beaten egg and brown under the grill.

Food for thought

✦ Remember a time when you waited for something you really wanted – a present, a person, a holiday, etc. What did it feel like?

✦ What do you like about being a member of the Church community and why?

✦ Tell the story of your life from your earliest memories to the present day. Where does God's story fit into your story? Where does your story fit in with stories in the Bible?

Easter Day

Background

This is the most important and joyful day in the Christian year. It is the Feast of the Resurrection of Christ, and is the most ancient feast of the Church. Because Easter Day always falls on a Sunday, each one is counted as a 'little Easter' – a day on which we celebrate and worship, rest and recreate.

There are 50 days of the Easter Season, the colour of which is white or gold. At the end of the 50 days the Church celebrates Pentecost, or to give it another name, Whitsunday. Included in this chapter are some things we like to do as a family to mark this important festival.

Bible readings

Year A	Year B	Year C
Jeremiah 31.1-6	Isaiah 25. 6-9	Isaiah 65.17-25
Acts 10.34-43	Acts 10.34-43	Acts 10.34-43
Matthew 28.1-10	Mark 16.1-8	Luke 24.1-12
or use John 20.1-18		

Prayer

Lord of all life and power,
who through the mighty resurrection
  of your Son
overcame the old order of sin and death
to make all things new in him:
grant that we, being dead to sin
and alive to you in Jesus Christ,
may reign with him in glory;
to whom with you and the Holy Spirit
be praise and honour, glory and might,
now and in all eternity. Amen.

(Collect for Easter Day from *Common Worship*)

Colour: white or gold

Grace before a meal

Bless us, Lord,
And bless this food and drink
You who on this day rose to new life
and saved us from sin.
As you give us this food to share,
May we share in your eternal kingdom.
Amen.

Preparing the home

Easter Day should have all the elements of celebration to accompany your Easter lunch. Just as we might take greater care over setting the table for Christmas lunch with napkins, candles, wine and so forth, we should do the same for this day.

Use the decorated white tablecloth (p. 44), along with the best crockery and napkins, and perhaps a bowl of spring flowers, and the tone will be set. A large candle can be bought in white or gold to signify Easter Day and this could burn for the 50 days of Easter at each meal time.

Activities
Easter egg hunt

It's always fun to hide smaller Easter eggs around the garden, if you have one and the weather is fine, or indoors throughout the house, for the children to find.

Go for a walk

If the weather is fine and sunny, go for a walk looking for signs of new life and appreciating God's creation!

Thoughts for food

Here are two recipes you may like to try for Easter Day. Chicken is traditionally served on Easter Day, usually roasted. This recipe adds a new twist to an old favourite. Also, for dessert there is a traditional Russian Easter dish, pashka.

Herby chicken pieces

4 x 175 g (6 oz) chicken breasts, skinned and boned
50 g (2 oz) seasoned flour
1 medium egg, beaten
75 g (3 oz) golden breadcrumbs
1 tbsp dried mixed herbs
1 tbsp olive oil
25 g (1 oz) butter

1. Cut the chicken into bite-sized pieces.
2. Mix together the breadcrumbs and the herbs.
3. Coat the chicken with the seasoned flour and dip in the beaten egg, then dip into the breadcrumbs and coat well.
4. Next, heat the oil and butter in a frying pan. When hot, fry the chicken in batches for about 7 minutes, or until golden. Serve immediately.

Pashka

Unless you have a special wooden Russian pashka mould, you will need a 15 cm (6 in) clay flower-pot, scrubbed and baked in a hot oven for 30 minutes, or a 1 kg (2 lb 2 oz) yoghurt pot with some holes pierced in the bottom.

You will need:
2 egg yolks
75 g (3 oz) vanilla sugar, or caster sugar and a few drops of vanilla extract
4 tbsp single cream or creamy milk
100 g (4 oz) unsalted butter, softened
700 g (1½ lb) curd cheese
50 g (2 oz) whole candied peel, chopped
50 g (2 oz) chopped blanched almonds

To decorate:
crystallized fruits

1. Beat the egg yolks in a bowl with the sugar until pale and foamy.
2. Then heat the cream or milk in a saucepan to just below boiling point, and add to the egg yolks. Stir well.
3. Return the mixture to the saucepan and stir until thickened. This takes only a moment, so watch it carefully: the mixture must not boil, or it will curdle. Remove from the heat and set aside to cool.
4. Beat the butter until light and creamy, then gradually beat in the egg yolk mixture.
5. Continuing to beat, add the curd cheese, a little at a time, then add the chopped peel and almonds.
6. Line the flower-pot or yoghurt carton with a double layer of kitchen paper, to extend over the top. Spoon the pashka mixture into the lined mould and smooth the surface, then fold the ends of the kitchen paper over the top. Put a small plate on top and weigh it down with scale weights or a heavy tin. Stand the pashka on a plate to catch any moisture that seeps out of the base.
7. Refrigerate for 6–8 hours or overnight. To serve, invert the container onto a serving dish, turn out the pashka and remove the kitchen paper. Decorate with crystallized fruits. (Rose Elliot, *Supreme Vegetarian Cookbook*, Fontana, 1990)

Food for thought

✦ If you had been there when Jesus arose from the dead what would you have said and done?

✦ What makes you full of joy? What can we do and say to bring joy to others?

✦ Do you think God has a sense of humour? Who and what do you think God laughs with and at?

Ascension

Background

Forty days after Easter Day we celebrate another festival of Revelation – the Ascension of Christ into heaven. The disciples of Jesus experienced his healing, his love, his forgiveness. After the Resurrection, Jesus told them that they would still experience him even though they couldn't see him. The Ascension shows us that we can know God even though we cannot see him.

Bible readings

Acts 1.1-11
Ephesians 1.15-23
Luke 24.44-53

Prayer

Grant, we pray, almighty God,
that as we believe your only-begotten Son
   our Lord Jesus Christ
to have ascended into the heavens,
so we in heart and mind may also ascend
and with him continually dwell;
who is alive and reigns with you,
in the unity of the Holy Spirit,
one God, now and for ever. Amen.

(Collect for Ascension Day from *Common Worship*)

Grace before a meal

Bless our home, Father,
that we cherish the bread before there is none,
discover each other before we leave,
and enjoy each other for what we are,
while we have time. Amen.

(J. Carden, comp., *Another Day*)

Preparing the home

As preparation for Ascentiontide, buy helium-filled balloons, heart shaped if possible, and tie them on to the back of dining chairs. Write on the balloon a word or words to complete the phrase 'Love is . . .'. If balloons are not available you could cut out heart shapes from red card, large enough to be used as a placemat. Give everyone felt-tip pens or crayons and get them to think about a word or words to write on their heart shape, to complete the phrase 'Love is . . .'.

Activity

Around the meal-table discuss a possible act of kindness or love or forgiveness that each could undertake. Carry this out during the ten days of Ascensiontide.

Thoughts for food

Ascension cake

You will need:

200 g (7 oz) packet of shortcrust pastry
4–6 tbsp mincemeat or jam
125 g (4 oz) glacé cherries, chopped
50 g (2 oz) sultanas
50 g (2 oz) ground almonds
185 g (6½ oz) sponge mix, plus ingredients to make up
1 tbsp ground almonds

1. Preheat the oven to 190°C (375°F, gas mark 5).
2. Roll out the pastry to a rectangle slightly larger than the tin. Line the tin, easing the pastry gently into the corners.
3. Prick the base thoroughly with a fork and remove the excess pastry with the rolling pin. Chill for 10–20 minutes, if you have the time.
4. Spread the pastry base with the mincemeat or jam and cover with the cherries, sultanas and flaked almonds.
5. Make up the sponge mix as directed and add the ground almonds.
6. Spoon the mixture into the pastry case and bake for 35–40 minutes, until golden and just firm. Cover the cake if it is browning too much.
7. Cut the cake into squares or fingers and serve warm or cold, sprinkled with sugar.

Food for thought

✦ When have been your own ascension times that you have experienced acts of love, care, forgiveness and healing?

✦ What happened at these times?

✦ Remember a time when you were forgiven. What was it and how did it make you feel?

Pentecost

Colour: red

Background

Pentecost falls ten days after Ascension Day and 50 days after Easter, and marks the time when the disciples received the gift of the Holy Spirit. You can read about this in Acts 2.1. It is sometimes referred to as the birthday of the Church. It is also known as Whitsunday, as traditionally baptisms took place on this day, at which white gowns were worn.

Bible readings

Year A	Year B	Year C
Acts 2.1-21	Acts 2.1-21	Acts 2.1-21
1 Corinthians 12.3b-13	Romans 8.22-27	Romans 8.14-17
John 20 .19-23	John 15.26-27	John 14.8-17

Prayer

God, who as at this time
taught the hearts of your faithful people
by sending to them the light of your Holy Spirit:
grant us by the same Spirit
to have a right judgement in all things
and evermore to rejoice in his holy comfort;
through the merits of Christ Jesus our Saviour,
who is alive and reigns with you,
in the unity of the Holy Spirit,
one God, now and for ever. Amen.

       (Collect for the Day of Pentecost from *Common Worship*)

Vigil Service

This Vigil Service should take place on the eve of Pentecost – the Saturday before Pentecost Sunday. A candle is lit with the words:

Come, Holy Spirit and burn as a flame in our hearts.

Reader 1: On the day of Pentecost God's Spirit came upon the disciples. We wait, as those disciples did, for the wind of heaven to blow within us.

All: **Come, Holy Spirit.**

Reader 2: On the day of Pentecost the disciples were changed from those who fled for fear to those who were fired with God's voice. We ask for boldness to speak God's word.

All: **Come, Holy Spirit.**

Reader 3: On the day of Pentecost the disciples were set free to love as God required. We ask for freedom to love our neighbours as ourselves.

All: **Come, Holy Spirit.**

Reader 4: On the day of Pentecost the disciples' hearts were set to serve you in their various gifts. May our gifts be used for your work.

All: **Come, Holy Spirit.**

Reader 1: Let us thank God for the gifts that make us who we are. Let us pause in silence . . .

Reader 2: For the gift of life.

All: **We thank you.**

Reader 3: For the gift of love.

All: **We thank you.**

Reader 4: For the gift of strength.

All: **We thank you.**

Reader 1: For the gift of joy.

All: **We thank you.**

Reader 2:	For the gift of peace.
All:	**We thank you.**
Reader 3:	For the gift of faith.
All:	**We thank you.**

Pause in silence.

Reader 4:	Let us offer to God in prayer those things which are in our hearts, spoken or unspoken.
Reader 1:	Let us say the Grace together:
All:	The Grace of our Lord, Jesus Christ, and the love of God and the fellowship of the Holy Spirit be with us all, evermore. Amen.

Grace before a meal

May the presence of Christ
bless our table
and the peace of Christ
be the fruit of our sharing. Amen.

Preparing the home
Make a Pentecost mobile

Find a place in your home to hang a mobile; it could be in a hallway or at the top of the stairs where it catches the breeze. Cut out dove shapes in silver, white or red. Cover a hoop in white or red crepe paper and hang streamers from it, and then hang the dove shapes in between. This can then be hung in your chosen space.

Activity
Make a kite

If it's a fine breezy day, go kite flying – watch the effects of the wind on trees, paper in the street and so on. You will need:

plastic or paper
two thin sticks 66 cm and 56 cm long
string
plastic or paper for the tail
sellotape
marker pens
scissors.

Measure 20 cm down from the top of the longest stick and attach it to the middle of the shorter stick with tightly wound string. Place the sticks on the plastic or paper and sellotape down. Next, mark straight lines between the ends of the sticks on the paper or plastic and cut out the kite shape. Now you need to attach a tail at least 140 cm long. Attach the length of string securely to the middle of the cross piece. Write a prayer on a piece of paper and stick it to the kite. You can also decorate it with the symbols of Pentecost – flames and a dove.

Wear something red – a red jumper, red socks, red ribbons, or just red shoelaces!

Thoughts for food

A birthday cake for the Church

Bake or buy a simple victoria sponge and cover it with fondant icing – the ready-roll packs are easiest. Colour the icing red and cover the cake. Roll out some white icing and, using a cardboard template in the shape of a dove, cut out the shape in white ready-roll icing. Place the shape on top of the cake and decorate with silver balls and a candle.

Fresh fruit salad

Whilst working on it, discuss the different fruits – although all different they come together to make one dessert.

Food for thought

✦ Remember a time when you were frightened. What happened next? How were you led from fear to trusting?

✦ Find out how the other people in your family pray. When do they pray and how do they do it? How can we help one another pray?

✦ God's spirit is known as a friend, a comforter, and the one who makes holy the people of God. How can we be these things for others? Where can we see the work of the Spirit in our own life?

Trinity Sunday

Colour: gold or white

Background

Trinity Sunday is the Sunday after Pentecost. This day reminds us that we worship one God whom we experience and come to know as Father, Son and Holy Spirit. In our family we like to think about relationships with family and friends as a way of reflecting on the relationship between the Trinity. One of the ways that this can be done is by making a family tree. The idea for this can be found in 'Preparing the home'.

The keynote of today is the praise of God who is in the relationship Father–Son–Spirit, and who invites us to be partakers in that divine life.

Grace before a meal

Praise God from whom all blessings flow,
Praise him all creatures here below,
Praise him above the heavenly host,
Praise Father, Son and Holy Ghost. Amen.

(Thomas Ken (1637 – 1711))

Bible readings

Year A	Year B	Year C
Isaiah 40.12-17,27-31	Isaiah 6.1-8	Proverbs 8.1-4,22-31
2 Corinthians 13.11-13	Romans 8.12-17	Romans 5.1-5
Matthew 28.16-20	John 3.1-17	John 16.12-15

Preparing the home
A family tree

You will need:

a large sheet of paper or thin card (wallpaper would do) about A4 size or larger

scissors, glue, pencils, felt-tip pens
sheets of white paper or photographs of family members.

On your large sheet of paper you will need to draw the outline of a tree.

Prayer

Almighty and everlasting God,
you have given us your servants grace,
by the confession of a true faith,
to acknowledge the glory of the eternal Trinity
and in the power of the divine majesty
   to worship the Unity:
keep us steadfast in this faith,
that we may evermore be defended from all
   adversities;
through Jesus Christ your Son our Lord,
who is alive and reigns with you,
in the unity of the Holy Spirit,
one God, now and for ever. Amen.

(Collect for Trinity Sunday from *Common Worship*)

You could then colour in the trunk and leafy part of the tree appropriately using felt-tip pens or poster paints if you prefer. If you have photographs of family members you could begin to stick them on, beginning with grandparents, then parents, then children. If you don't have photos then perhaps a drawing to represent that person could be stuck on instead. Display your family tree in a place where you meet and eat.

This activity is more suited to younger children. Older children would probably enjoy researching their family tree in the more conventional manner, talking to older relatives and gathering the information and any old photographs that grandparents or others may have.

Activity
Prayer mobile

You will need:

an old wire coathanger
string or wool, and scissors
paper or thin card, and felt-tip pens
photos of family or pictures of things or activities associated with them, e.g. a grandmother who enjoys gardening could be represented by a picture or postcard of flowers or a garden from a gardening catalogue.

Decide on the family members (and friends) you want to include in your mobile and find appropriate pictures or photos to represent them. Then glue your pictures onto a piece of card, leaving a border around your picture.

Make a small hole in the top and thread a piece of string or wool through. Next, tie the other end of the string on to the wire coat-hanger. Make the string of varying lengths, and write the person's name in bold letters on the back of the card. Put more string around the hook part of the wire coathanger and hang it up in an appropriate place – children's bedroom, lounge, etc. It should look something like this:

Help your children to think and pray for the people on their mobile.

Thoughts for food
A three-coloured jelly

You will need:

3 packets of jelly, each of a different colour, e.g. one red, one yellow, one green
hot water and a measuring jug and spoon
chilled water from the fridge
a large glass bowl big enough to hold 1½ litres (3 pints).

Make up one packet of jelly according to the manufacturer's instructions. When it has dissolved pour it into the bowl and leave it to set in the fridge. Make the other packets of jelly up one after the other, allowing the previous jelly to set before pouring the second and third on top. When you make up the other two jellies use half the amount of boiling water and allow the jelly to dissolve thoroughly, then make up the full amount of liquid to one pint by using chilled water from the fridge. This should cool the jelly down so that the jelly underneath won't melt too much. Pour it on top very gently or ladle it on carefully before it sets. If you have sundae glasses you could try making individual Trinity jellies.

Food for thought

◆ In what way is God a friend to you?

◆ God the Father, Son and Spirit are friends. How is their friendship seen in your life? How do you carry this into your own friendship?

◆ Think about your family. A family is God's way of saying . . .

Corpus Christi

Colour: white

Background

Corpus Christi is the Latin name for the body of Christ. This day falls on the Thursday after Trinity Sunday, and is a day when we thank God for the institution of Holy Communion. As a family we bake bread at Corpus Christi because it is a staple food. When we eat it we can think of the other ways in which we are fed and nourished by God. This leads us to think how we can be 'bread' for others.

Bible readings

Genesis 14.18-20
1 Corinthians 11.23-26
John 6.51-58

Prayer

Lord Jesus Christ,
we thank you for the gift of yourself.
Give us grace
that we may know within ourselves
and show forth in our lives
the fruits of your love.
For you are alive and reign with the Father
in the unity of the Holy Spirit
one God, now and forever. Amen.

Grace before a meal

The bread is warm and fresh
The water cool and clear
Lord of all life, be with us,
Lord of all life, be near. Amen.

(Everyday Graces)

Activities

The coffee chain game

This game can be used by adults and older children. It helps us to become aware of how we are physically fed and the values we hold as Christians in the world. You will need:

a 100 g jar of coffee, price marked as £1.60
a copy of the grid shown on the next page, drawn on a flipchart or chalkboard with the proportion column hidden
a photocopy of the role cards (shown on pages 57-8) for each group

1. Split the players into five groups and give each group its role card.
2. Give each group a short time to think about their role. What sort of problems might they face? What strengths do they have?
3. Hold up the jar of coffee, priced at £1.60. How much of its selling price does each group think it should get for the work they have done?
4. Each group takes a turn to tell the rest how much they should get. Encourage them to justify their claim. Record each amount in the 'initial proportion' column of the grid.
5. Add up the amounts in that column – they may well come to more than £1.60! The groups now negotiate until the total reaches £1.60. Encourage discussion, discourage violence!
6. When agreement is (finally) reached, record the figures in the 'negotiated proportion' column.
7. Finally, reveal the 'actual proportion' column to show the figures different groups would receive.
8. Allow plenty of time for discussion after this role-play and encourage the children to empathize with the real people involved in the coffee trade.

	INITIAL PROPORTION	NEGOTIATED PROPORTION	ACTUAL PROPORTION
Growers			8p
Exporters			8p
Shippers			£1.04 (Shared)
Roasters			
Retailers			40p

Role cards

Give a card to each person (text from *Value and Visions*, Christian Aid, 1993).

Coffee growers

You live in a rural part of southern Uganda. You have about two acres of land to farm and your main source of income is from growing and selling coffee. You plant the coffee trees and weed the ground. The trees require lots of regular work and attention to keep them healthy so they bear fruit well. You harvest the coffee 'cherries' by hand when they are ripe. You dry them in the sun and sell them to a visiting buyer. The money you earn from the coffee is essential to pay for your children's school and the family's medical bills. Every 15 years you need to buy seedlings to replace old trees.

Coffee exporters

You visit the growers to buy their coffee. The growers are scattered over a wide area, so you have to pay for transport and fuel to collect the coffee. Your factory processes the coffee 'cherries' to extract the 'green beans'. You sort the beans, pack them in bags, and transport them to the coast where you sell them to a shipping company. Uganda is landlocked and so you have to pay high rail freight charges. The market for coffee is unpredictable, so you sometimes have to pay to have it stored. You also need money to renew and repair expensive machinery in the factory and to pay skilled people to operate it.

Shipping companies

You buy the bags of 'green' coffee beans from the coffee exporter, load them on to your ship, and transport them to the UK where you sell them to the coffee roaster. You have to pay highly skilled personnel to operate your ships. There are risks involved and you have to take out insurance for the ships and their cargoes, as well as pay for fuel. You also need to pay fees for using the ports, and taxes for importing the coffee.

Roasters

You buy the 'green' coffee beans from a shipping company and mix the different varieties of bean to get a 'blend'. You roast the beans and process them to make instant coffee then package it into jars and sell it to the retailers. It is a very competitive business and so you have to spend large amounts of money to advertise your brand and to provide attractive packaging. You constantly need to invest money to improve the taste of your blend and keep ahead of the competition.

Retailers

You buy the instant coffee from a wholesaler (the roaster). You store it until you need it, label it with the price, put it on display and sell it to the customer. You have to pay high rents to sell your goods at a busy location. You have to make your shop attractive, which means expensive decoration, and you need to train and pay a large sales force to provide a good service to the customer.

Thoughts for food

Caribbean bake – a bread for Corpus Christi

You will need:

    450 g (1 lb) plain white flour
    1½ tsp baking powder
    50 g (2 oz) butter
    a pinch of salt
    half a 375 g (15 oz) can of coconut milk
    water

1. Sieve the flour, baking powder and salt together into a large mixing bowl.
2. Rub in the butter.
3. Make the coconut milk up to 300 ml (½ pint) by adding the water and stirring.
4. Make a well in the dry ingredients and add the coconut mixture. Stir it into the flour to form a soft dough.
5. Knead lightly on a floured surface but don't overhandle the mixture.
6. Shape into a 20 cm round and place on a greased baking tray. Prick all over with a fork and bake in the oven at 200°C (400°F, gas mark 6) for 30–40 minutes, or until the bread sounds hollow when tapped on the bottom.
7. Cool on a wire tray and eat on the day of making.

Food for thought

✦ In the Lord's Prayer we pray 'give us this day our daily bread'. What are our daily needs for our mind, body and spirit? How can we share this 'bread' with others?

✦ What has to change for the world to be a better place?

✦ When is God near to us?

Petertide

Background

The 29th June is the day when we remember the apostle Peter. It is through him that God worked, so that the gospel message could be proclaimed to the whole world. Jesus gave Simon the name Cephas or Peter which means rock. Jesus said to Peter 'You are Peter and on this rock I will build my church . . . I will give you the keys of the kingdom of heaven'. He ended his journey in Rome where he died. The symbol for St Peter is a set of keys. We sometimes throw a Petertide party and invite friends to join in.

Bible readings

Zechariah 4.1-6a,10b-14
Acts 12.1-11
Matthew 16:13-20

Prayer

Almighty God,
who inspired your apostle Saint Peter
to confess Jesus as Christ and Son of the
    living God:
build up your Church upon this rock,
that in unity and peace it may proclaim one
    truth
and follow one Lord, your Son our Saviour
    Christ,
who is alive and reigns with you,
in the unity of the Holy Spirit,
one God, now and for ever. Amen.

(Collect for Peter from *Common Worship*)

Grace before a meal

This is sung to the tune of 'Top Cat'.

Top nosh! The most incredible
Top nosh! That's ever fed to me
Breakfast through 'til dinner and tea,
All my friends can share it with me . . .

Top nosh! So tasty it could be
Straight from heav'n above
Thank you God, as you guide,
And for all you provide –
Food and fellowship . . . and love!

(from *Reign Dance*)

Preparing the home

Petertide is traditionally the time when the Church ordains deacons and priests. It is a time when the Church looks at what it proclaims and how God calls. We can echo this theme in the home by giving a party and inviting family and friends. The following activities and food can all be used to help the party go with a swing!

Petertide net

You will need:

    a large sheet of red crepe paper
    red balloons
    paper
    pencils
    scissors
    string, drawing pins or Blu-Tack.

To make the net fold the crepe paper lengthways so that it makes a strip about 10 cm wide. Make cuts three-quarters of the way into the strip at 5 cm intervals. Repeat along the opposite side.

Unfold the crepe paper and tie a length of string to each corner. Gently pull the paper to form a net. Tie up on the ceiling, ready to take the balloons.

Cut the paper into strips 1 cm x 20 cm. Take a verse from a favourite hymn or song and write one sentence on one piece of paper. Carefully roll it up and insert into one balloon. Inflate the balloon and tie it off. Continue until all the hymn or song has been used.

The example below may help:

1. Will you come and follow me
   If I but call your name?
   Will you go where you don't know
   And never be the same?
   Will you let my love be shown
   Will you let my name be known
   Will you let my life be grown
   In you and you in me?

2. Will you leave yourself behind
   If I but call your name?
   Will you care for cruel and kind
   And never be the same?
   Will you risk the hostile stare
   Should you life attract or scare?
   Will you let me answer prayer
   In you and you in me?

3. Will you let the blinded see
   If I but call your name?
   Will you set the prisoners free
   And never be the same?
   Will you kiss the leper clean
   And do such as this unseen
   And admit to what I mean
   In you and you in me?

4. Will you love the 'you' you hide
   If I but call your name?
   Will you quell the fear inside
   And never be the same?
   Will you use the faith you've found
   To reshape the world around
   Through my sight and touch and sound
   In you and you in me?

5. Lord, your summons echoes true
   When you but call my name
   Let me turn and follow you
   And never be the same
   In your company I'll go
   Where your love and footsteps show
   Thus I'll move and live and grow
   In you and you in me.

('The Summons' from *Heaven Shall Not Wait*)

Place all the balloons in the net. At an appropriate point in the party either jump to knock the balloons out or release the net. Then burst the balloons to reveal the paper strip inside. As a group try to piece together the verse of the hymn or song in the correct order. When it is complete you can sing it!

Activity

St Peter ended his travels in Rome having shared the Good News upon the way. The house hunt party game follows a modern day journey from Jerusalem to Rome, calling at some capital cities. The object of the game is to find the approximate distances between the capital cities that have been hidden around the home. The first to collect all distances is the winner. You will need:

Blu-Tack
pens and pencils
11 small strips of paper
copies of the following sheet for all the players.

Before the game begins the distance between two capital cities needs to be written on a strip of paper. Repeat for all the other cities. You should have eleven strips as follows:

1. Jerusalem–Amman, 120 km (75 miles)
2. Amman–Damascus, 240 km (150 miles)
3. Damascus–Beirut, 150 km (94 miles)
4. Beirut–Ankara, 500 km (312 miles)
5. Ankara–Athens, 750 km (470 miles)
6. Athens–Tirane, 450 km (280 miles)
7. Tirane–Sarajevo, 250 km (156 miles)
8. Sarajevo–Zagreb, 250 km (156 miles)
9. Zagreb–Ljubljana, 125 km (78 miles)
10. Ljubljana–Bern, 450 km (280 miles)
11. Bern–Rome, 600 km (375 miles)

(all distances are approximate)

These eleven strips should be hidden around the home. Each player or team is given a pen and a copy of the sheet:

Jerusalem–Amman (Jordan)
Amman–Damascus (Syria)
Damascus–Beirut (Lebanon)
Beirut–Ankara (Turkey)
Ankara–Athens (Greece)
Athens–Tirane (Albania)
Tirane–Sarajevo (Bosnia Herzegovina)
Sarajevo–Zagreb (Croatia)
Zagreb–Ljubljana (Slovenia)
Ljubljana–Bern (Switzerland)
Bern–Rome (Italy)

TOTAL

The first to fill in all the distances and add them up to 3885 km (2426 miles) is the winner!

Thoughts for food
Banana boat

You will need for each boat:
2 wafers
1 large banana
1tbsp lemon juice
4 scoops ice cream
150 ml (¼ pt) double cream, whipped, or aerosol cream
chocolate sauce
1 tbsp hundreds and thousands.

1. Cut the wafers in half diagonally.
2. Cut the banana into two, lengthways, and brush the halves with lemon juice.
3. Place the scoops of ice cream on a long plate, and press the banana halves along either side of the ice cream.
4. For the whipped cream, put a large star-shaped nozzle into a piping bag, then spoon in the cream and pipe over the ice cream. Alternatively, squirt aerosol cream over.

5. Dribble chocolate sauce over and sprinkle with hundreds and thousands.
6. Finally, push the wafers into the cream and serve immediately.

Fish bites

You will need:

> 1.25 kg (2 lb) sole or any firm white fish, filleted and skinned
> plain flour for coating
> 2 medium eggs, beaten
> 175 g (6 oz) fresh breadcrumbs
> oil for deep frying

1. Cut the fish into 1cm x 4 cm strips.
2. Coat the fish in flour, then dip it into the beaten egg and roll in the breadcrumbs. Chill for about 30 minutes.
3. Heat the oil until very hot. Lower the fish into it, about eight strips at a time, and cook until browned. Drain on paper towels and keep warm in the oven at a very low temperature.
4. Serve with a dip made with soured cream and lump fish roe.

Food for thought

✦ Name a person you know who is like Jesus and say why.

✦ What does being a follower of Jesus mean in your everyday life?

✦ When you feel loved what does it make you want to do?

The Transfiguration

Colour: white

Background

The 6th August marks another festival of the Revelation of God. Jesus, Peter, James and John went up a mountain to pray. Whilst there, Jesus' appearance changed and he was clothed in light. Moses and Elijah appeared with Jesus and God the Father declared that Jesus was his Son. Those with him saw the light and it became a turning point in their lives.

The Transfiguration of Jesus shows us that when we meet the Revelation of God we shall have our lives changed.

Grace before a meal

Come, Lord Jesus, be our guest,
and may our meal by you be blest. Amen.

(attributed to Martin Luther, 1483–1546)

Bible readings

Daniel 7.9-10, 13-14
2 Peter 1.16-19
Luke 9.28-36

Activity

Intercessions book

You will need:

paper
pens
postcards
photographs
magazine pictures
scissors
glue.

Prayer

Father in heaven,
whose Son Jesus Christ was wonderfully transfigured
before chosen witnesses upon the holy mountain,
and spoke of the exodus he would accomplish at Jerusalem:
give us strength so to hear his voice and bear our cross
that in the world to come we may see him as he is;
who is alive and reigns with you,
in the unity of the Holy Spirit,
one God, now and for ever. Amen.

(Collect for the Transfiguration of Our Lord from *Common Worship*)

First of all you will need to sit down as a family and decide on the subjects or people for which you want to pray. Make your prayers as simple as possible, e.g. 'God, please help us to take care of the world'.

Write this out on a piece of A4 paper and then choose a picture to cut out and glue underneath.

You could compose five or six prayers (or more if you want) and then bind them together and add a suitable cover, or alternatively place them in a ring-binder to add to later.

On or about the Transfiguration we like to take our prayers out with us and visit a hill or high place. There we use the prayers.

4. Add the ground almonds and lemon rind and mix well to make a firm dough. Then wrap in clingfilm and refrigerate for 30 minutes.
5. Preheat the oven to 175°C (350°F, gas mark 4) and grease several baking sheets.
6. Divide the dough into 32 equal pieces.
7. Roll each piece into a strip 10 cm long and place it on the baking sheet. Then bring the ends together to form a circle and pinch together.
8. Bake for 15 minutes until very lightly browned.
9. To glaze, place the honey in a small saucepan and warm it. Brush the biscuits with the honey and sprinkle with flaked almonds. Next, return them to the oven for approximately 2 minutes.
10. Cool on baking sheets for a few minutes then remove to wire racks to cool completely.

Thoughts for food

Biscuits for the Transfiguration

100 g (4 oz) softened butter
50 g (2 oz) caster sugar
1 medium egg, beaten
225 g (8 oz) plain flour
50 g (2 oz) ground almonds
grated rind of 1 lemon

For the glaze:
2 tbsp honey
2 tbsp flaked almonds

1. In a bowl beat together the butter and sugar.
2. Gradually beat in the egg.
3. Sieve the flour onto the creamed mixture and mix in.

Food for thought

✦ If Jesus was with you now, what would he say?

✦ Think of the times that you feel close to God. When are they and why?

✦ At what moments in our lives does the love of God shine through us?

Michaelmas

Background

The 29th September is the Feast of St Michael and All Angels. Throughout the Bible there are instances of God's angels bringing messages to people and praying for them. The name Michael is the English form of a Hebrew name which means 'who is like God?' It was Michael who drove Lucifer from heaven. There are three other archangels, one of whom is Gabriel, who appeared to Mary to tell her she would be the mother of Jesus. He also appeared to the shepherds to announce the birth of Jesus. Raphael, who God sent into the world to heal, cares especially for those who travel and for children, and Uriel was sent by God to warn Noah of the flood. He is known for his wisdom and can see into the future.

Bible readings

Genesis 28.10-17
Revelation 12.7-12
John 1.47-51

Prayer

Everlasting God,
you have ordained and constituted the ministries
of angels and mortals in a wonderful order:
grant that as your holy angels
    always serve you in heaven,
so, at your command,
they may help and defend us on earth;
through Jesus Christ your Son our Lord,
who is alive and reigns with you,
in the unity of the Holy Spirit,
one God, now and for ever. Amen.

(Collect for Michael and All Angels
from *Common Worship*)

Grace before a meal

For food in a world where
many walk in hunger;
For faith in a world where
many walk in fear;
For friends in a world where
many walk alone,
We give you humble thanks
O Lord. Amen.

(Girl Guide World Hunger Grace)

Preparing the home
Angel decoration

You will need:

card
scissors
pens and glitter to decorate.

Cut out the shape as illustrated, making a slit at point B. Place tab A into the slit.

This angel decoration could be used as a place setting by writing the person's name on the front, or several of them could be strung onto a mobile or simply hung up above your child's bed.

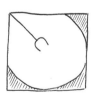

Activity

Design for a letter

Angels bring messages and so, during Michaelmas, our activity is to design and print an edging for a letter.

You will need:

a piece of A4 paper, any colour you prefer

half a potato.

Very carefully cut out your desired shape,

(very young children will need help).

If you prefer you could use string glued onto a piece of card,

Alternatively, there are printing blocks available from craft shops.

Using poster paints brush the paint onto the surface of your shape and print around the edge of the paper to create a border. We try to encourage our children to write a letter to someone to say thank you or get well or simply to send good news. You could also decorate the back of the envelope when you've sealed the letter inside.

Thoughts for food

Traditionally in some parts of England the 29th of September is the last day to pick blackberries. The devil is said to have spat them out as he was cast out of heaven into hell by St Michael. Here is a recipe for Michaelmas tart using blackberries and apples.

Michaelmas tart

350 g (12 oz) rich flan or shortcrust pastry
6 apples, peeled, cored and sliced
225 g (8 oz) blackberries
2 tbsp sugar
½ tsp cinnamon
125 g (4 oz) unsalted butter, chopped
175 g (7 oz) plain flour
4 tbsp soft brown sugar
4 tbsp sesame seeds

1. Preheat oven to 190°C (375°F, gas mark 5).
2. Roll out the pastry on a lightly floured surface and use it to line a swiss roll tin or other rectangular tin. Trim the top edges of the pastry and prick the base with a fork.
3. In a saucepan, mix the apples, blackberries, sugar and cinnamon with 1 tbsp water. Cook for 5 minutes, or until the fruit is soft but still holds its shape. Cool the fruit and set aside.
4. Using a slotted spoon, put the fruit mixture on top of the pastry base.
5. In a bowl, rub together the butter and flour until the mixture resembles fine breadcrumbs, and add the brown sugar and sesame seeds.
6. Sprinkle the mixture over the fruit and bake for 35–40 minutes.
7. Serve hot or cold, sprinkled with more sugar.

Food for thought

✦ Think of a person or situation that shows you something of God.

✦ Think of someone who needs your prayers at this time and say why. Include them in your daily prayers.

✦ Think of a place or situation in your life or the world that needs God's healing. Offer these to God in your prayers.

All Saints and All Souls

Background

On All Saints Day, 1st November, we celebrate the saints and heroes of our faith – those women and men throughout the centuries whose lives show us something of God. All Souls, or the Commemoration of the Faithful Departed, follows on the 2nd November. On this day we remember our own departed friends and relatives.

Bible readings

All Saints – 1st November

Year A	Year B	Year C
Revelation 7.9-17	Isaiah 25.6-9	Daniel 7.1-3,15-18
1 John 3.1-3	Revelation 21.1-6a	Ephesians 1.11-23
Matthew 5.1-12	John 11.32-44	Luke 6.20-31

All Souls – 2nd November

Lamentations 3.17-26,31-33

Romans 5.5-11

John 5.19-25

Prayers

All Saints

Almighty God
you have knitted together your elect
in one communion and fellowship in the
    mystical body of your Son Christ our Lord:
grant us grace so to follow your blessed saints
in all virtuous and godly living
that we may come to those inexpressible joys
that you have prepared
    for those who truly love you;
through Jesus Christ you Son our Lord,
who is alive and reigns with you,
in the unity of the Holy Spirit,
one God, now and forever. Amen.

(Collect for All Saints' Day from *Common Worship*)

All Souls

Eternal God, our maker and redeemer,
grant us, with all the faithful departed,
the sure benefits of your Son's saving passion
    and glorious resurrection
that, in the last day,
when you gather up all things in Christ,
we may with them enjoy the fullness of your
    promises;
through Jesus Christ your Son our Lord,
who is alive and reigns with you,
in the unity of the Holy Spirit,
one God, now and for ever. Amen.

(Collect for the Commemoration of the
Faithful Departed from *Common Worship*)

Grace before a meal

This is sung to the tune of 'Addams Family'.

(Da da da da click click …)
O Lord, we're really grateful
for every cup and plateful
forgive us when we're wasteful
coz we're your family.
You guide us and you lead us
you strengthen us and feed us
to live and love like Jesus
coz we're your family!
(da da da da Thank God!)

(from *Reign Dance*)

Activities

Paperchain saints for 1st November

You will need:

> a piece of plain paper 10 cm x 60 cm
> scissors
> pens, crayons and felt-tip pens to decorate.

Concertina the paper into 7 cm widths, leaving 2 cm at the beginning and end of the paper. On the first 7 cm section, draw the outline of a person making sure that the hands touch the edges of the paper. Whilst still folded, cut around the outline. Open up to reveal eight paper people holding hands! Decorate the paper people, including the names of the family members and the names of some saints. Place Blu-Tack on the 2 cm strips at either end of the chain and place it where it can be seen.

Remembrance candle for 2nd November

You will need:

> a large candle
> paper
> pens
> scissors.

Cut a large circle from the paper and stand the candle in the middle. Write or draw on the paper the names of all we remember who have died. As they are remembered, recall something about each person who is dear to you. Close the activity with a prayer.

Thoughts for food

Gingerbread saints

You will need:

> 200 g (7 oz) plain flour
> 2 tsp ground ginger
> 1 tsp mixed spice
> ½ tsp bicarbonate of soda
> 75 g (3 oz) soft brown sugar
> 75 g (3 oz) butter
> 2 tsp of golden syrup
> currants
> tubes of coloured icing

1. Heat the oven to 200°C (400°F, gas mark 6).
2. Sieve together the flour, mixed spice, ginger and bicarbonate of soda into a bowl.
3. Put the sugar, butter and syrup in a saucepan and heat until the butter is melted and the syrup is runny.
4. Pour the mixture into the bowl of dry ingredients and mix together into a dough.
5. Allow to cool and become stiffer.
6. Put the dough onto a floured surface and roll out to ½ cm thick.
7. Using a gingerbread-man cutter, cut out as many gingerbread men as you can.
8. Put the gingerbread men onto a baking tray covered with greaseproof paper, putting on currants for the eyes and nose.
9. Bake for 10–15 minutes until golden brown in colour.
10. Remove from the oven and leave to cool.

When the gingerbread people are completely cold you can use the tubes of icing to write the names of saints onto them. You could take this as an opportunity to learn about the lives of some of the saints. There are many books available that can provide stories and information – choose your favourite or find out about your own name-saint.

Soul cakes

Soul cakes are a traditional recipe at this time of year. While the cakes are being prepared, begin a discussion about who are the heroes of faith and also those who have died known only to us. It has been the custom for people, especially young people, to go from house to house singing the following song with the expectation of being given a soul cake:

> A soul, a soul, a soul cake
> Please good missus, a soul cake.
> An apple, a pear, a plum or a cherry
> Any good thing to make us all merry.
> One for Peter, two for Paul
> Three for Him who made us all.

To make soul cakes you will need:

450 g (1 lb) strong white flour
1 tsp salt
1 tsp mixed spice
½ tsp ground ginger
1 tsp cinnamon
50 g (2 oz) butter
25 g (1 oz) fresh yeast
40 g (1½ oz) sugar
300 ml (½ pint) milk
honey and demerara sugar

1. Heat your oven to 220°C (425°F, gas mark 7).
2. Mix the flour, salt, mixed spice, ginger and cinnamon together in a large bowl.
3. Rub in the butter and leave in a warm place for a while.
4. Now mix the yeast and sugar together gently in a separate bowl and leave for a few minutes until frothy, then add the yeast mixture and milk to the flour. This should be worked into a dough.

5   Knead the dough for about 5 minutes, then cover with a cloth and leave in a warm place for an hour, until doubled in size.
6. When the dough has risen turn it out on a floured surface and knead it again.
7. Divide the dough into ten or twelve portions and roll each into a ball. Flatten the balls and place them on a floured baking tray.
8. Leave the buns again for about 20 minutes, until well risen, and then bake for about 20 minutes.
9. When the buns are cooked, warm some honey in a saucepan and brush it over them whilst they are still warm, then sprinkle them with demerara sugar.

Food for thought

✦   Think about the people you know who show us something of what God is like. These people might have one or all of the following qualities: those who are loving, show mercy, seek for truth, have a love of justice, work to overcome conflicts and help to make peace. What do you most admire about the person and why?

✦   Name as many saints as you can. Try to recall something about their life and what they did for God.

✦   God calls ordinary people to be his saints. In what ways are our lives an example to others? What can we do to live a more God-centred life?

Christc the King

Background

On the Sunday before Advent we celebrate Christ the King. This is the final Sunday of the Church's year. Christ rules as king over an inclusive kingdom, which has at its heart the gospel themes of sacrificial love, truth, justice, freedom, reconciliation and peace.

Grace before a meal

The eyes of all look to you, O Lord, and you give them their food in due season. You open your hand And fill all things living with your bountiful gifts. Amen.

Bible readings

Year A	Year B	Year C
Ezekiel 34.11-16,20-24	Daniel 7.9-10, 13-14	Jeremiah 23.1-6
Ephesians 1.15-23	Revelation 1.4b-8	Colossians 1.11-20
Matthew 25.31-46	John 18.33-37	Luke 23.33-43

Preparing the home

We enjoy eating slices of crown cake and encourage our children to use the mealtime to help and serve each other at the table. We think also of ways in which we can be of service in places outside our home.

Prayer

Eternal Father,
whose Son Jesus Christ ascended to the
  throne of heaven
    that he might rule over all things as Lord
    and king:
keep the Church in the unity of the Spirit
and in the bond of peace,
and bring the whole created order to worship
    at his feet;
who is alive and reigns with you,
in the unity of the Holy Spirit,
one God, now and for ever. Amen.

(Collect for Christ the King from *Common Worship*)

Activities
Christ the King placemats

To make these placemats you will need:

a piece of A4 card for each member of your family
shiny/foil paper in gold
silver or bronze
glue
scissors.

Cut a simple crown shape out of foil paper and glue it onto the A4 card. Write the owner's name in bold letters and then decorate the crown with paper shapes. Sometimes photographic shops will laminate items like this. This will protect the surface and give you longer use.

We like to use these placemats at mealtimes throughout the week following the feast of Christ the King, but during that time we try to place even greater emphasis on serving one another at mealtimes, passing bowls and plates, fetching and carrying and taking it in turns to be of service to one another and encouraging our children to continue this in their daily lives.

Prayer rope

The idea for a prayer rope is an ancient one. A knotted rope has been used for many centuries as an aid to prayer. Each knot along the rope represents one prayer. It may be the same prayer repeated, or it may be different prayers. To begin using the prayer rope you may like to use the Jesus prayer:

> Jesus Christ
> Son of God
> have mercy on me
> a sinner.

The words are said quietly and slowly, paying attention to your breathing and the volume of sound made. There are ten knots on the rope, which can be used to say the prayer ten times. As one person at prayer time in the family finishes the round of ten, others may wish to say their own round of ten. Once you become accustomed to saying this, or other prayers in this way, you may find you will be carried in prayer with the rhythm and calm that it creates.

For the prayer rope you will need:

a length of string, wool or thin rope 30 cm long for each person
an optional small cross with loop for attachment to the rope.

While leaving 3 cm at either end of the rope, make ten large knots with even spaces between each one. Tie both ends together, including the cross, and trim the excess. The prayer rope is ready for use!

Thoughts for food
Crown cake

For the cake:
175 g (6 oz) butter, at room temperature
175 g (6 oz) caster sugar
3 medium eggs
125 g (4 oz) self-raising flour
50 g (2 oz) ground rice
1/4 tsp almond essence

For the sides:
1 tbsp apricot jam or marmalade (sieved)
250 g (8 oz) packet of marzipan

For the top of the cake:
75 g (3 oz) glacé cherries, quartered
25 g (1 oz) angelica, cut into small leaves
25 g (1 oz) mixed chopped peel
40 g (1 1/4 oz) sultanas
25 g (1 oz) flaked almonds
50 g (2 oz) butter
25 g (1 oz) caster sugar
1 tbsp brandy
3 glacé cherries, halved, for the sides

1. Set the oven at 160°C (325°F, gas mark 3). Grease and base-line a deep sponge or shallow cake tin 20.5 cm (8 in) across.
2. In a bowl beat together the sugar and butter until soft and fluffy.
3. Beat in the eggs one at a time, adding a spoonful of flour with the third egg.
4. Stir in the remaining flour, ground rice and almond essence.
5. Spread the mixture in the prepared tin and bake in the centre of the oven for 50–55 minutes. Test by pressing lightly in the middle – when the cake is cooked it should feel springy and also be easing away from the sides of the tin.
6. Allow to cool for 10 minutes, then turn out on a wire rack.
7. Spread the jam or marmalade around the sides of the cake.

8. Roll out the marzipan to a strip that covers the sides and press it firmly into position. (This is a generous amount of marzipan for the depth of the cake.)

9. For the top, melt the butter gently in a pan and stir in the sugar and brandy.

10. When the sugar has dissolved, add the fruit and nuts and heat for a few minutes, stirring carefully until they are all well coated and the juices have been absorbed.

11. Dip the halved cherries in the glaze and press them onto the marzipan at intervals.

12. Leave the fruit and nut mixture until cooled and then arrange it to cover the top of the cake.

Food for thought

✦ Where at school, at work, in the home or in church do you see signs of sacrificial love, truth, justice, freedom, reconciliation and peace?

✦ List all the words given to describe Jesus. What sort of a king is Jesus if these are the words we use to describe him?

Further Liturgies

Welcoming home a new-born baby

The family gathers round the crib or cot in which the baby is lying.

Leader: You, Lord, are the source of all life.

All: Glory to you, O God.

Leader: You have given us _____ (name the baby).

All: Glory to you, O God.

Leader: You share with us the work of creation.

All: Glory to you, O God.

Leader: Let us remember how God, in Jesus, came into the world as a baby.

A reading: The shepherds hurried away and found Mary and Joseph, and the baby lying in a manger. When they saw the child they repeated what they had been told about him, and everyone who heard it was astonished at what the shepherds had to say. As for Mary, she treasured all these things and pondered them in her heart. And the shepherds went back glorifying and praising God for all they had heard and seen. (Luke 2.16-20)

A prayer: With joy, Lord, we lovingly welcome _____ into his/her home. May he/she feel safe here and know that he/she is loved by us all. Touch this young life with love, with beauty and with the wonder of living. Amen.

All join together in saying the Christian family prayer:

Our Father in heaven,
hallowed be your name,
your kingdom come,
your will be done,
on earth as in heaven.
Give us today our daily bread.
Forgive us our sins as we forgive those who sin against us.
Lead us not into temptation,
but deliver us from evil.
For the kingdom, the power and the glory are yours,
now and for ever. Amen.

Leader: Angels sang at the birth of Jesus.

All: We celebrate the birth of _____.

Leader: Shepherds marvelled at the birth of Jesus.

All: We celebrate the birth of _____.

Leader: Wise men knelt in worship before Jesus.

All: We celebrate the birth of _____.

As everyone stretches out a hand over the baby the Leader says:

May the joy of the angels, the enthusiasm of the shepherds, the perseverance of the wise men and the peace of the Christ child be with you, _____ , and remain with you always. Amen.

Extra readings: 1 Samuel 1.27-28, the birth of Samuel

While the blessing is being said you may prefer everyone to touch the baby – or the leader may sign him/her with a cross.

Baptism anniversary

You will need:

a jug of water and an empty bowl
a candle (if possible, the one given at baptism)
matches or a lighter.

The jug of water, the bowl and the candle are placed on a small table or stool where everyone can see them. As water is poured into the bowl:

Leader: For your gift of water

All: **We thank you, Lord.**

Leader: For the water of baptism,

All: **We thank you, Lord.**

As the candle is lit:

Leader: For your gift of light which guides us and warms us,

All: **We thank you, Lord.**

Leader: For the light of Christ,

All: **We thank you, Lord.**

The lighted candle is given either to the person whose baptism is being remembered or to a god-parent, as someone says:

This is to remind us that, in baptism, _____ passed from darkness to light, and is to shine as a light in the world to the glory of God the Father.

A reading: You are a chosen race, a royal priesthood, a holy nation, God's own people, that you may declare the wonderful deeds of him who called you out of darkness into his marvellous light. (1 Peter 2.9)

A prayer: Lord God our Father, we thank you that, by your Holy Spirit, _____ has been born again into new life and received into the fellowship of the Church. Grant that he/she may grow in the faith into which he/she has been baptized and that all things belonging to the spirit may live and grow in him/her. Amen.

Everyone gathers round the person whose baptism is being remembered (together, where appropriate, with a godparent) as all say:

The grace of our Lord Jesus Christ and the love of God and the fellowship of the Holy Spirit be with us all evermore. Amen.

The candle is blown out and greetings exchanged.

You might like to read a few verses from one of the following:

Deuteronomy 30.15-20	life or death; blessing or curse
Ezekiel 36.4-8	a new heart and a new spirit
Mark 1.4-8	John baptizes
Matthew 3.13-17	Jesus is baptized
John 3.1-8	being born again
Romans 6.3-4	buried and raised with Christ.

When the water is poured into the bowl, some may like to dip their fingers in and sprinkle the water, or sign themselves or the one whose baptism is being remembered with the sign of the cross.

Birthday

You will need a candle and some matches or a lighter. The candle is placed on a small table, stool or box around which the family can gather. As the birthday person lights the candle everyone sings:

Happy Birthday to you!
Happy Birthday to you!
May God richly bless you
Another year through.

Everyone greets the birthday person.

Leader: Thank you, God, for this special day.

All: Thank you, God.

Leader: For your love which lasts for ever,

All: Thank you, God.

Leader: For the love which joins us together,

All: Thank you, God.

A reading: You know all about me O God – when I'm resting, when I'm working. You are wherever I am. If I climb the skies or explore the underworld, you are there! If I fly with the sun from dawn to dark, your hand is still on my shoulder. Darkness is no darkness to you; night is as bright as day, darkness as light! You made me the person I am. You've known what I am really like from the moment I was born. You've seen me grow up; no day has passed by uncounted or slipped by unnoticed. What you think of me matters to me, O God, more than anything else. (From Psalm 139 in *Winding Quest* by Alan Dale)

A prayer: Thank you, Father, for _____ and for all he/she means to us. Help him/her and all of us to love you more and to grow in love for one another. We ask this through Jesus Christ our Lord. Amen.

Leader: May almighty God bless us, the Father, the Son and the Holy Spirit.

All: Amen.

The candle is blown out.

Starting a new term

You will need a table on which are placed a school bag for each child and a variety of objects representing different aspects of school life, e.g. book, pen, lunch box, and football boots. The family gathers round the table.

Leader: To the new term ahead of us,

All: We look forward with hope.

Leader: To the lessons we shall take part in and the games we shall play,

All: We look forward with hope.

Leader: To the friends we shall met,

All: We look forward with hope.

Leader: To all who will care for us,

All: We look forward with hope.

A prayer: Your world, O Lord, is great and wonderful and we have much to learn. Be with us as we start this new term. Help us not to be afraid of new things. Make us more loving and truthful, and more caring about one another. We ask this through Jesus Christ our Lord. Amen.

A reading: Always be happy in the Lord. Be gentle and kind. Don't worry about anything. Pray and ask God for everything you need. And when you pray, always give thanks. Then God will give you peace. Think about good things. Think about what is true, honourable, right, pure, beautiful and praiseworthy. God will be with you if you do. (From Philippians 4, *International Children's Bible*)

A prayer: Lord Jesus, you called together your disciples so that they could learn from you and then teach others. Thank you for our teachers and for all the other people who work in our school. Help us, with all of them, to make our school a happy place. Amen.

Leader: God be in my head and in my understanding.

All: **Be with me in this new beginning.**

Leader: God be in my eyes and in my looking.

All: **Be with me in this new beginning.**

Leader: God be in my mouth and in my speaking.

All: **Be with me in this new beginning.**

Leader: God be in my heart and in my thinking.

All: **Be with me in this new beginning.**

Each child puts his/her belongings in his/her bag.

Leader: Send us out, O Lord, in the power of your Spirit, to live and work to your praise and glory. Amen.

If the closing words are familiar to everyone, all may join in.

Wedding anniversary

You will need photograph(s) of the wedding and/or a recent photograph of the couple. The photographs are put on a small table or stool, where everyone can see them.

Leader: Let us praise the Lord, together;

All: **He watches over our lives.**

Leader: Our help comes from the Lord;

All: **He watches over our lives.**

Leader: The Lord himself is our keeper;

All: **He watches over our lives.**

Leader: The Lord will defend us from all evil;

All: **He watches over our lives.**

A reading: In marriage, husband and wife belong to one another, comforting and helping each other, living faithfully together in need and in plenty, in sorrow and in joy. They begin a new life together in the community. It is a way of life that all should honour. (Adapted from the prologue to the Marriage Service.)

Leader: Let us each, in silence, thank God for the comfort, help and love that _____ and _____ have brought to each other, to us and to many other people through their marriage.

A reading: Love is patient and kind; love is not jealous or boastful; it is not arrogant or rude. Love does not insist on its own way; it is not irritable or resentful; it does not rejoice at wrong, but rejoices in the right. Love bears all things, believes all things, hopes all things, endures all things. Love never ends. (1 Corinthians 13.4-8)

A prayer: God our Father, you have taught us through your Son that love is the fulfilling of the law. Grant to your servants that, loving one another, they may continue in your love until their lives' end; through Jesus Christ our Lord. Amen.

Leader: Now let us go forth in the love of the God the Father.

All: **Amen.**

Leader: In the love of the Son who lived, died and rose again for us;

All: **Amen.**

Leader: In the love of the Holy Spirit who inspires and sustains us;

All: **Amen.**

Everyone greets the celebrating couple. If a video was made of the marriage service, all or part of it could be played before this liturgy. You might like to keep two wine glasses for the celebration of the wedding anniversary. If so, have them ready, filled, on the table or stool, with the photographs. Husband and wife can then drink to each other.

You might like to read a few verses from one of the following:

Ecclesiastes 4.9-12   two are better than one
Romans 12.9-13   let love be genuine
Colossians 3, 12-17   put on love
1 John 4.7-11   let us love one another.

You might like to sing one of the hymns you sang at your wedding.

When someone we care about is in hospital

You will need a photograph of the sick person and/or some object that reminds you of him or her (perhaps a present they have given). The

photograph and/or objects should be placed on a small table or stool around which the family can gather.

Leader: To you, Lord, we come in all our need.

All: **In you we trust.**

Leader: To you we bring our prayers for _____ .

All: **In you we trust.**

Leader: In fear and hope, in joy and pain,

All: **In you we trust.**

A prayer: Father, your Son showed how much you love when he cared for the sick and the weak. In our love for _____ we come to you. Stay close to him/her to heal and strengthen and give him/her again the joy of your help. We ask this in the name of Jesus Christ. Amen.

A reading: Is any one among you suffering? Let him pray. Is any cheerful? Let him sing praise. Is any among you sick? Let him call for the elders of the church, and let them pray over him, anointing him in the name of the Lord; and the prayer of faith will save the sick man, and the Lord will raise him up. (James 5.13-15)

Prayers: Father, we thank you for all who are caring for _____ ; for all the doctors and nurses, for those who prepare food and medicine, for the cleaners and all others who help to make the hospital run smoothly. Help them to be patient and loving, and give them the joy of knowing that they are working with you. We ask this through Jesus Christ our Lord. Amen.

Give strength, Lord, to all _____'s closest relations and friends, so that they can cheerfully face the extra worries they have, in the power of Jesus Christ. Amen.

Leader: Lord, you hold us all together in love.

All: We hold each other in love.

Leader: Your love spans the distance between us.

All: We hold each other in love.

Join hands and say together:

The grace of our Lord Jesus Christ and the love of God and the fellowship of the Holy Spirit be with us all evermore. Amen.

Remembering a death (or the anniversary of such a death)

You will need a candle and some matches or a lighter; each person will need to bring a photo or object that reminds them of the person who has died.

A candle is put on the table around which the family can gather. The candle is lit and people place around it the photo or object they have chosen to bring, explaining briefly, if they wish, why they made this choice.

Leader: God is our refuge and strength; a very present help in trouble.

All: Lord we trust you.

Leader: Therefore we will not fear though the earth be moved and the mountains shake in the midst of the sea.

All: Lord we trust you. (Psalm 46.2)

Leader: Wait for the Lord; be strong and take courage.

All: Lord, we trust you. (Psalm 27.14)

A reading: St Paul wrote, 'We know that he who raised the Lord Jesus will raise us also with Jesus and bring us, with you, into his presence. So we do not lose heart. Though our outer nature is wasting away, our inner nature is being renewed every day. We know that, if the earthly tent we live in is destroyed, we have a building from God, a house not made with hands, eternal in the heavens'. (from 2 Corinthians 4 and 5)

Keep a few moments of silence for reflection.

Prayers: Thank you, Lord, for the life of _____ and for all he/she means to us. Thank you for a life well lived, for love shared and for kindness shown. As we treasure his/her memory, may his/her goodness and love continue to inspire us to greater heights of living and loving, through Jesus Christ, our Lord. Amen.

Help us, Lord, to use aright the time that is left to us here on earth: to remember the needs of others, to serve and help those in trouble and so to live, that we may not be afraid to die. Through Jesus Christ, our Lord. Amen.

Leader: You, Christ, are the king of glory, the eternal Son of the Father.

All: You are the Lord of heaven and earth.

Leader: You overcame the sting of death and opened the kingdom of heaven to all believers.

All: You are the Lord of heaven and earth.

Leader: Bring us, with your saints, to glory everlasting.

All: You are the Lord of heaven and earth.

Join hands together and say:

The grace of our Lord Jesus Christ and the love of God and the fellowship of the Holy Spirit be with us all evermore. Amen.

The candle is blown out and people reclaim their possessions. You might like to read a few verses from one of the following:

Psalm 18	the Lord is my rock
Psalm 90	a thousand years in your sight are but as yesterday
Psalm 91	the Lord guards those who trust in him
Matthew 11.28-30	come to me all who are heavenly laden
John 14.1-7	in my Father's house are many rooms
Revelation 21.1-7	God will wipe away every tear.

If you enjoy singing you might like to include a favourite Easter hymn or one of the verses of Psalm 23, 'The Lord is my shepherd'.

New Year

You will need a candle and some matches or a lighter, a calendar (or diary) for the New Year, wrapped up, and a calendar (or diary) for the past year.

Leader: Lord, you have been our refuge from one generation to another.

All: **Lord, you have been our refuge.**

Leader: A thousand years in your sight are like yesterday, passing.

All: **Lord, you have been our refuge.**

Leader: Teach us so to number our days that we apply our hearts to wisdom.

All: **Lord, you have been our refuge.**

A prayer: Thank you, Lord, for the year that has gone – for the things we have enjoyed doing, for people to love and for those who love us, for our health and safety, and for all that has in any

way helped us to grow. Through Jesus Christ, our Lord. Amen.

The candle is lit as someone reads:

I said to the man who stood at the gate of the year, 'Give me a light that I may tread safely into the unknown'. And he replied, 'Go out into the darkness and put your hand into the hand of God. That shall be to you better than light and safer than a known way.' So I went forth and, finding the hand of God, trod gladly into the night. (M. Louise Haskins)

As the old calendar is thrown away:

Lord, as we throw away this calendar, we ask you to forgive all the wrong things we thought, or said, or did last year – and all the good things we meant to do, but left undone. Help us to forgive each other and to leave behind all unfriendliness. For Jesus Christ's sake. Amen.

As the calendar for the New Year is unwrapped:

We make a new beginning with Jesus, who said, 'Behold, I make all things new'.

Leader: We look forward to the New Year hopefully.

All: **We trust in your love.**

Leader: We make one resolution – to seek each other's happiness.

All: **We trust in your love.**

Leader: Lord, help us to share your peace.

All: **We trust in your love.**

The candle is blown out. You might like to read a few verses from one of the following:

Joshua 1.1-9	be strong and courageous
Joshua 24.15-24	choose this day whom you will serve
Psalm 91	the Lord guards those who trust him
Romans 8.28-39	assurance for the future
Philippians 3.12-14	pressing on towards the goal
Hebrews 12.1-3	running the race.

(all from Diocese of Birmingham, *Home Liturgies* pack)

Appendix 1

The lectionary year

Church year	Lectionary year
(Advent to Advent)	
1999/2000	B
2000/2001	C
2001/2002	A
2002/2003	B
2003/2004	C
2004/2005	A
2005/2006	B
2006/2007	C
2007/2008	A
2008/2009	B
2009/2010	C
2010/2011	A
2011/2012	B
2012/2013	C
2013/2014	A
2014/2015	B
2015/2016	C
2016/2017	A
2017/2018	B
2018/2019	C
2019/2020	A
2020/2021	B
2021/2022	C
2022/2023	A
2023/2024	B
2024/2025	C

Appendix 2

The date of Easter and accompanying festivals

Year	Ash Wednesday	Easter Day	Ascension Day	Pentecost (Whitsunday)	Advent Sunday
2000	8 March	23 April	1 June	11 June	3 December
2001	28 February	15 April	24 May	3 June	2 December
2002	13 February	31 March	9 May	19 May	1 December
2003	5 March	20 April	29 May	8 June	30 November
2004	25 February	11 April	20 May	30 May	28 November
2005	9 February	27 March	5 May	15 May	27 November
2006	1 March	16 April	25 May	4 June	3 December
2007	21 February	8 April	17 May	27 May	2 December
2008	6 February	23 March	1 May	11 May	30 November
2009	25 February	12 April	21 May	31 May	29 November
2010	17 February	4 April	13 May	23 May	28 November
2011	9 March	24 April	2 June	12 June	27 November
2012	22 February	8 April	17 May	27 May	2 December
2013	13 February	31 March	9 May	19 May	1 December
2014	5 March	20 April	29 May	8 June	30 November
2015	18 February	5 April	14 May	24 May	29 November
2016	10 February	27 March	5 May	15 May	27 November
2017	1 March	16 April	25 May	4 June	3 December
2018	14 February	1 April	10 May	20 May	2 December
2019	6 March	21 April	30 May	9 June	1 December
2020	26 February	12 April	21 May	31 May	29 November
2021	17 February	4 April	13 May	23 May	28 November
2022	2 March	17 April	26 May	5 June	27 November
2023	22 February	9 April	18 May	28 May	3 December
2024	14 February	31 March	9 May	19 May	1 December
2025	5 March	20 April	29 May	8 June	30 November

Appendix 3

Resources

Bibles and Bible stories

Pat Alexander, *The Puffin Children's Bible*, Penguin, 1981.

Jeff Anderson and Mike Maddox, *The Lion Graphic Bible*, Lion, 1998.

The Dorling Kindersley Illustrated Family Bible, Dorling Kindersley, 1997.

Children's Illustrated Bible, Dorling Kindersley, 1998.

Joyce Ellis, *The One Minute Children's Bible*, Hodder & Stoughton, 1993.

Good News Bible, published by The Bible Societies, Collins/Fontana, 1976.

The Great Bible Discovery Series, M. Publishing, 1995.

Holy Bible – New International Version Children's Edition, Hodder & Stoughton, 1994.

Noah's Ark, *David and Goliath*, *The Birth of Jesus* and *The Miracles of Jesus*, Dorling Kindersley, 1996.

Brian Ogden, *Bible Stories for Young Readers*, On the Story Mat series, Barrabas, 1998.

Brian Ogden, *Bible Stories for 6–8 Years*. Just Time to Catch the Post series, Barrabas, 1999.

David Pickering, *Bible Questions and Answers*, Dorling Kindersley, 1997.

V. Rees, *The Toddlers Bible*, Victor, 1992.

Rob Suggs, *The Comic Book Bible*, Barbour, 1995.

Youth Bible – New Century Version, Nelson World Bibles, 1993.

Prayer books for children

Joyce Denham, *A Child's Book of Celtic Prayers*, Lion, 1998.

Christopher Herbert (compiler), *Pocket Prayers for Children*, NS/CHP, 1999.

Christopher Herbert (compiler), *Prayers for Children*, NS/CHP, 1993.

A. & C. Parry, *The Bible Made Easy: A Pop-up, Interactive Bible*, Hunt & Thorpe, 1999.

Lois Rock, *All Year Long: Anytime Prayers for Little Children*, Lion, 1997.

Lois Rock (compiler), *Glimpses of Heaven: Poems and Prayers of Mystery and Wonder*, Lion, 1987.

Rachel Stowe, *Children at Prayer*, Marshall Pickering, 1996.

Carol Watson, *365 Children's Prayers*, Lion, 1989.

Carol Watson (compiler), *Prayers for a Fragile World*, Lion, 1997.

Books on prayer and worship

Helen Albans, *Praying with Sticky Fingers: Down to Earth Prayers for Parents and Young Children*, Methodist Church Division of Education, 1992.

Elizabeth Brimelow, *In and Out the Silence*, Quaker Home Service, 1989.

Ruth Cardwell, *Helping Children to Pray*, A Grail Publication, 1981.

Stephen Cottrell, *Praying Through Life: How to Pray in the Home, at Work and in the Family*, NS/CHP, 1998.

Anne Evans, *Room for God*, NS/CHP, 1996.

Christine Hall and Judy Jarvis, *Milestones: Marking Important Events for Children and Parents*, Methodist Church Division of Education, 1993.

Susan Harriss, *Jamie's Way: Stories for Worship and Family Devotion*, Cowley, 1991.

Nancy Marrocco, *Homemade Christians: A Guide for Parents of Young Children*, Collins, 1987.

Jenny Pate, *Praying with Children*, McCrimmons, 1995.

Madeleine Simon, *Born Contemplative: Introducing Children to Christian Meditation*, DLT, 1993.

Graces

Everyday Graces, Lion, 1993.

Pat Fairon, *Irish Blessing*, Appletree Press, 1996.

A. & L. Perry, *Mealtime Prayers* (boardbook), Hunt & Thorpe, 1995.

Pam Robertson (compiler), *Pocket Graces*, NS/CHP, 1994.

Games

Bible Baffle, Talicor Inc., 1996.

Bible-Op, a cooperative game for kids, 1–4 players aged 3+, Late for the Sky Production Co.

Bibleopoly, a biblical game of fun and faith for 2–6 players aged 8+, available from Bible Lands Trading Ltd, Tel: 01494 521351.

Bible Trivia II, a game for 2–4 players aged 8+, or teams, Cadaco.

Celebrating Families, card game, available from The Dawn Project, 95–99 Effingham Street, Rotherham, S65 1BL.

The Family Dinner Game, a 'getting to know you' game that helps families communicate better, available from the Family Caring Trust, 44

Rathfriland Road, Newry, Co. Down, BT34 1LD, Tel: 01693 64174.

God Loves Me, card game, Candle Books, 1996.

Audio cassettes

Feeling Good: Songs of Wonder and Worship for 5's and Under, Church House Publishing, 1994.

Hymns for Children, EMI, 1992.

The Lion Storyteller Bible, Lion, 1995.

Psalms for Singing, Pilgrim Tapes, 1995 (available from Pilgrim Tapes, PO Box 409, Harrow, HA2 6HZ).

CD ROMs

Just Like You, twelve original songs for children of all ages, Gloryhouse!, 1997.

Read with Me Bible, for ages 5–10, Hodder & Stoughton, 1997.

Videos

Adventures in Odyssey, animated series from Focus on the Family Films, 1991.

Bledlow Ridge, live action from Lantern Production, 1996 (Tel: 01892 52651).

The Greatest Adventure, stories from the Bible, animated series by Hanna Barbera, 1995.

Roly's Old Testament Takes, available from Focus TV, 1998 (Tel: 01703 448822).

The Story Keepers, animated series by SP Media, 1997.

Testament : The Bible in Animation, S&C/Christmas Films, 1996.